THE TOP REALTOR SECRETS YOU CAN'T AFFORD TO MISS

In memory of the generations of
African Americans,
Native Americans,
Africans,
Asians
and other cultures who were beaten,
murdered and/or barred from
purchasing a home because of racist
laws, evil customs, ignorance, and
other social forces.

The Top Realtor Secrets You Can't Afford To Miss

Tricks Of The Trade To Make More Money Selling Your Home

DONALD DRAKE

World of Learning Publishing

Copyright

Published by World of Learning Publishing Group (PO Box 181, Anaheim CA 92815). Library of Congress Cataloging-in-Publication Data is available upon request. No part of this book may be reproduced, shared, stored in a retrieval system or transmitted by any means without the written permission of the author.

First Edition.

Print ISBN: 978-0-578-24802-8
Ebook ISBN: 978-0-578-91389-6

Contents

COMMON SELLER MISTAKES

8
LEARN FROM OTHER'S MISTAKES

9
FINDING PRECIOUS BUYERS

10
BE A POWER NEGOTIATOR

11
THE DO'S AND DON'TS OF NEGOTIATING

12
KNOW YOUR BARGAINING CHIPS

13
WHY HIRE A REAL ESTATE PRO?

Biography

Born in Wichita Kansas and raised in Riverside California with 4 of 5 siblings (all girls!). As a child, I had aspirations of being a fair, decent and reasonable Judge - however, I did not want to be an Attorney, which presents obvious problems.

Never in a million years did I think I would stumble into the real estate industry, in fact I didn't even know there was such a thing, but after having a son and wanting, rather needing to be a full time Dad, I left a great career at the boutique investment firm, Smith Barney Harris & Upham.

I wish I could tell you an inspirational and sweet story about how I came to a career in real estate, but in this life, you can't always direct or predict where or when you'll discover what you love to do. Be flexible.

I was taught at a young age that if you want something in life, you have to work for it; and most cases, you have to work 2x harder than the people around you. So, since the age of 12, that is what I did; work. We had a great upbringing on Kathleen street. From teachers like my parents Bill and Joyce Drake, my Uncle William, Grand Daddy Jonny Fisher, Carleton Reed, Dell Roberts, Mr. Oliver – and as a beginning Realtor I had great teachers like

John Chesshire and Jolene O'signac at the Shire, Marsha Miller, Rich Cosner, plus many college business & finance courses – I learned to work hard, be smart and do the right thing, the foundation of good business.

I pulled weeds, cut grass, painted, learned to stucco and do roofing, trim trees and anything else I could think of or that came up, including as an adult, Insurance, Medicare Heath Insurance, Finance, Investing and of course, the Real Estate businesses. At least I know that if I ever ran into "problems," I'm not afraid of, and know how - to work.

I've sold Millions & Millions of dollars of real estate but this "about me" will be the very short story because Realtists & Realtors are taught to focus and highlight themselves, which I find self-serving, boring and unnecessary. As an Agent, you either care about your clients or not. And as a client, the agent either does his job well, or not. The rest is just words. Just talk. And we hate talkers.

It's really that simple. "Give to get; the more you give, the more gifted you become." After making the decision to be a "full time" Dad and leaving a great job working for Bill Barney, V.P. at Smith Barney. I had to find something that would give me the flexibility to both raise my son and earn a decent wage.

[side note: Bill Barney was no revolutionary or civil or employment activist of any kind but just a cool and very decent human. Through him, I was exposed to a different world in some ways - that my parents and grandparents were restricted from. With no special motives, he gave me opportunity - that others in that "Brentwood" all male & all white world would not have. I learned practical investing application, "Pop Stocks," what moved a stock and what didn't; he didn't know it, but he changed my life. He was a good friend to me.] So here we are 20+ years later....

The main advantage of hiring me? Clients got a true advocate, which means doing more than any other agent would do, to achieve client goals (which includes more than anything you can think of, or than I can admit in writing). This is more than valuable when you have difficult tenants, a challenging property or legal issues in the transaction.

Throughout my career, I have earned numerous accolades that I won't list because they mean nothing to you. The aim is to provide the highest level of service to my clients and take deep pride in helping them achieve their real estate goals; no matter what it takes. This is what I want you to look for when it's time for you to pick your advocate.

Foreword

When I first ventured into the real estate industry back in June of 1998, I did so with the hopes of helping sellers like you avoid the headaches often associated with the home-selling process (in addition, I needed a job that would give me the flexibility to be hands on in raising my son Jelani who was just a little person at the time).

In my years of experience, not only have I helped numerous clients alleviate the stress of selling their home(s) but also accumulated years of knowledge to help sellers receive more money for their home in the least amount of time. If you are a For Sale By Owner, it can be done, but you are at a real disadvantage and really need to study these pages. As a seller or buyer, you can compare this advice with what your agent is telling you and make sure you're getting accurate information. Sharing my expertise and the most valuable insights with would be clients, buyers and sellers (and future Real Estate Agents who might consider this adventure as a career) is my ultimate goal.

And that is why you're receiving this book. I want to help you have the best possible home-selling experience. And by that, I mean I want you to:

1. Get the most money possible for your home
2. Learn the short cuts to make the process more efficient and less stressful
3. Sell in the least amount of time, and
4. Avoid the headaches most commonly associated with the home-selling process

Think of this book as my gift to you. It contains insider advice on the home-selling process to help you achieve your ultimate real estate goals, including:

· Secret strategies to sell your home for more money
· Marketing techniques employed by top agents
· Advice on how to appeal to today's buyers
· And much, much more

If after reading through these pages if you would like assistance, I or someone on my team would be more than happy to consult with you by Zoom or in person to discuss a specific plan for your situation. I wish you great success.

Remember two things: It is vital to find an experienced Real Estate Agent (10 years+) who will put your needs and goals before all others to help you attain your goals and the most profit, *and* take a deep breath, carefully read through the steps in this book and know you will be fine.

Happy reading and go make some money!

D. Drake

1

First Steps To Home Selling

**"But You Gotta Know the Territory"
— and Terminology**

Location! Location! - Location! is the most crucial consideration in real estate and a major factor, if not the predominant one, in real estate pricing. Novice (and not-so-novice) home sellers alike must know the considerations that determine a home's price.

Setting the price at which to sell your home is not a simple formula, nor is it strictly mathematical and definitely not accurate if determined from an online algorithm. Many elements factor into the decision. Throughout this book, you will read examples of similar and similarly situated houses that sold for very different prices, along with the reasons for the disparities. A calculated home value is not necessarily what you believe your home is worth. Recognizing this helps avoid overpricing, a major factor that leaves homes languishing or unsold. Pride can be you biggest sin in pricing. Remember, you're moving, it's not "your home" anymore.

Familiarity with the real estate terms *market value, intrinsic value, appraisal value,* and *assessed value* can save disappointment & frustration, and allow the home seller to accurately engage in setting a home's listing price.

The most-used definition of *market value* is "the most probable price a property should bring in a competitive, open market under conditions requisite to a fair sale." Essentially, this is a pre-negotiation, opinion of what a house *should* bring in its local market, its geographical area, or generally an area such as a suburb or neighborhood usually withing one city mile of the subject property.

Appraisal value is an evaluation of a property's worth at a given point in time that is performed by a professional appraiser. Appraised value is a crucial factor in loan underwriting and determines how much money may be borrowed and under what terms. For example, the Loan to Value (LTV) ratio is based on the appraised value. Where LTV is greater than 80%, the lender generally will require the borrower to buy mortgage insurance. For example, if you put down 3%, the bank wants insurance protection on the mortgage, which is $200-$600 per month, on top of your house payment, paid by you.

Assessed value is the amount local or state government has designated for a specific property, it almost always differs from market value or appraisal value. This assessed value is used as the basis of property tax and when a property tax is levied. The assessed value of real property is not equal to the property's market value. Approximately 75% of U.S. properties are assessed lower than their current market value.

Intrinsic value is a measure of what an asset is worth, which may be more than its market value. This measure is arrived at by means of an objective calculation like average price per square foot and average price per ¼ acre, rather than simply using the current comps of that asset. For accurate pricing, you must estimate all of a properties future perceived values (eg., a new stadium or entertainment center being built nearby). Calculate and sum up the present value of each of these matrices to obtain the intrinsic value of the property, which equals: what the house is worth.

WHAT IS YOUR HOME WORTH?

The first step in selling your home is knowing the difference between *value, worth,* and *price.* Let's examine the determining factors at work. Understanding those factors allows them to be leveraged. There are several ways a home's value is derived.

ONLINE HOME VALUATION

Online tools will provide you with a very basic, (repeat: very basic) estimate of your home's current value based on recent comparable home sales in your area using a comprehensive database. Note that the assessment is based on available data with no guarantee of accuracy and often uses an algorithm that simply averages comparable sales in the geographic area. These tools are the quick and dirty, and they don't take into consideration factors like location, current local trends and the condition of the property. Companies like Zillow for example, are not real estate firms and their information is second or third hand, which could be old, not updated, delayed and inaccurate - but it does give you a good start.

For example, a home in Ohio was put into one such system, Redfin (https://www.redfin.com/what-is-my-home-worth). The home last sold for $180,000 in 1998; it was appraised for refinancing in 2015 at $275,000. In 2017, Redfin's calculator valued this 1890 Victorian home (4 bedrooms, 1.5 baths, and 2,100 square feet) in a four-block area of "Grand Old Ladies" at $158,000. The apparent reason is that the six "comps" (comparable recent sales) included only 2 homes in this desirable neighborhood (over $300,000), while four others outside this small neighborhood, although close, sold for $150,000 to $199,000. Because the system doesn't understand the makeup of the area and simply pulled prices from a broader geographic area, the arrived-upon price was far below what it should have been. These tools are worthwhile for obtaining "comps" of area sales; however, they are not highly accurate in arriving at a listing price.

** Secret **

These real estate services are great businesses. They pay the Realtor MLS for real estate information in order to provide it to you, to search their website. Then get Realtors to pay them to advertise next to that listing information because you are there, to get folks like you who are looking for homes to call them and hopefully become clients. Whew! But that's a big part of how they make money in their expanding business model.

Data does come from the MLS but being 2nd or 3rd hand, it is not always accurate and information on sales are not always updated or current, which is why you will find discrepancies. After all, it may be better to have more info than the most accurate, to work that type of online business. You be the judge.

EXAMPLE OF DIFFERING HOME VALUATIONS

A buyer is interested in a home listed at $1,400,000. The online valuation determines the house is worth $1,480,000. Based on that estimate, the buyer offers the asking price. When a professional appraisal comes in at $1,390,000, and the existing tax records assess the home at $1,275,000, the buyer, confused at all the numbers, wonders why the values are so different and whether he overpaid.

The house was listed at $1,400,000 because at that price, the home would sell in a reasonable amount of time. Why would the appraised value not be whatever a buyer was willing to pay? The fact that they paid $1,400,000 does not mean that is the true value of the home. Certain factors may weigh in — undesirable businesses located near the property, for example. Online valuations cannot take into consideration the condition of the property or the qualities of the neighborhood.

Since an assessed home value is for taxing purposes only, it can be much more or much less than the market value. Ideally, they should be the same but it's not an ideal world and usually they are not; it is based on a percentage of the appraised value determined by a professional which in itself is somewhat subjective. From legal descriptions to onsite inspections, to comparable home-selling prices, the assessor will take all these things into consideration when appraising a home. Location near industry, high traffic, or potential development will also positively or negatively affect the appraisal.

PROFESSIONAL APPRAISAL

Nothing determines the sale price of a piece of real estate but the price at which it *sells.* Houses are not same-priced identical cans of Tuna on the grocery store shelf or shares of stock valued and traded every day on the stock exchange.

Real estate appraisal ("property valuation") is the process of arriving at developing a perspective of value for real property. This is the *market value* — i.e., what a willing reasonable buyer would pay for the property to a willing reasonable seller. Real estate transactions generally require assessments because they happen infrequently, and every real property is unique in features and characteristics. Remember, it is a reasonable buyer to a reasonable seller. If you are an unreasonable seller, you may feel pleased or proud that your house is listed for $8 million but will you still be pleased a year later because it is a listing that no reasonable person wants to buy?

An appraisal helps in various decision points. The seller can use the appraisal as a basis for pricing. The buyer can use it as a gauge on which to base an offer. Lenders use appraisals to know how much money to loan to their borrowers.

The important factors in a house appraisal are:

- Dwelling type (e.g., one-story, two-story, split-level, factory-built)
- Features - structure, design and materials used
- Improvements made that add value to a house
- Comparable sales – Same size and condition, near by
- Location — type of neighborhood, zoning areas, proximity to other establishments
- Age of property, size, number of rooms

Condition, of course, is a crucial factor in valuation. Location is also a factor; however, as property cannot change location, upgrades or improvements to a residential property often can enhance its value. Which is more valuable to you? The best house in the worst neighborhood or the worst house in the best neighborhood? Like life, it's all a balance, you don't necessarily want to be at either extreme.

A professional appraiser should be a qualified, disinterested specialist in real estate appraisals, with expertise in your region. His or her job is to determine an estimated value by inspecting the property, reviewing the initial purchase price, all available data, and weighing it against recent sales with the same purchase price.

COMPETITIVE MARKETING ANALYSIS
BY A REAL ESTATE PROFESSIONAL

This home valuation is free from real estate professionals and more helpful than automated online offerings. It provides detailed information on each house sold in your area over the last three to six months, along with the final sale price. It also includes the specifics of all the *relevant* houses for sale in your area, including the asking price. These homes are your competition. The real estate professional will also answer any questions and help you price your home realistically.

Along with an understanding of how the worth of a home is determined, the current market must be considered. By utilizing an experienced professional real estate agent, you can rely on proven expertise to market your home at the best listing price. You can do your initial research at www.DDrakeRealEstate.com.

** Hot Tip **

Once you have decided to sell your home, stop think-ing of it as "your home" because it is, or soon to be, someone else's home. Instead of your home, it is now a house or property. You will earn more money on the sell - and actually sell the house, once you make this men-tal switch.

THE SECOND STEP

(SELLING YOUR *HOUSE* FOR MORE)

Prior discussion showed that there is no calculable certainty in setting the value of a home, or house. There can be wide differences between the seller's assessed price, the asking or listing price (market value), and the price at which the house sells (sale price). Let's turn to what the house seller can do to elicit offers at the listing price, or even above, in a competitive market.

The seller's time, effort, and investment are the most important parts of the process. The seller's willingness to adequately prepare the house for presentation by improving, freshening, landscaping, and generally making the house pristine — and to live in that presentation-readiness state for the time it takes to sell the property — will greatly affect both the sale period as well as the price at which the house sells.

A market in which a house normally sells in no more than six months of listing is considered balanced or neutral, which means a good number of house owners are selling and buyers are purchasing; therefore, neither has an upper hand. A variable, for instance, like a major company entering — or moving from — the area will tip the scale toward house owners to make a swift market or toward buyers to make a slow market. The typical selling time in a swift market might be 30 days, while that of a slow market may be up to nine months. Generally, any number below six months is considered a seller's market.

LIVING IN A SWIRLING FISHBOWL

A house on the market requires keeping the house in a constant "show-ready" condition, and adjustment to changes in day-to-day life that are inherent in the process. Sellers can get out-of-business-hours phone calls from unrepresented prospects and buyers' agents to show the house; frequent updates by phone, email, and text and show appointment scheduling messages from the listing agent; repair and reconditioning appointments; and inspections. The house may be pho-

tographed   for   online,   periodical,   or   brochure
presentations.

There are repeated showings when the house first hits
the market. Keep your house in pristine showing condition for impromptu visitors — the perfect prospect
might just drop in at dinnertime. Rude, perhaps, but necessary to accommodate. Don't forget you are selling your
house, it's part of the process.

*** Secret ***

*Open houses are a good way to let people come in all
at once to see the property however, it has very little
to do with actually selling your house. Only 1 in about
5,000 will actually buy the house they saw open. Brokers hold open house for two reasons.*

*1) Sellers think it will help sell their house and thus
expect several open houses*

*2) Open Houses help the Broker to market themselves
to find new buyers and sellers*

CHILDREN (AND PETS)
SHOULD BE UNSEEN & UNHEARD

Children and pets are distractions for potential buyers, affecting their experience in seeing your house.
Don't be offended, this is one of your largest business
transactions. Take it seriously. You should plan for your

children to be elsewhere and your pets crated or leashed, and no toys lying about or dog hair on the sofa. The dishes should always be done and the kitchen sparkling.

The pressure of showing to everyone even mildly interested in looking (not necessarily buying) may come from the idea that the more your house is seen, the more quickly and easily your house will sell. Many real estate agents provide their clients with dozens of houses to consider without a clear picture of what the buyer wants. Low-interest traffic can be heavy and a burden on the seller's time, energy, and resources.

Since a showing can take an hour or more, finding an interested buyer is what matters most. The house will be shown to many more uninterested than interested buyers. How many times will you have to show your house? In an ideal world, your property would be shown to serious buyers only. However, many "Sunday afternoon window shoppers" exist in the real estate business. Just like you, people like to look at homes and even dream a little. Most lookers are not even looking in their price range. People tend to look above what they can afford thus you do not want quantity. You want a Broker who will provide quality folks who might buy your house; but you never know.

You should not waste your time trying to appeal to uninterested buyers. This is where planning, organizing, and the professional help of a qualified real estate agent enables you to handle even the most intimidating tasks without wasting efforts.

Again, focus on your strengths and put your marketing efforts and attention where it will do you good, on your strengths, not what is common to every other house on the market.

2

Pareto's Principle

"Eighty percent of results will come from just twenty percent of the action." This is the Pareto principle, attributed to Italian economist and philosopher Vilfredo Pareto, who in 1906 observed an intriguing correlation. The story is that he began work on the "80/20 rule" with the observation that 20% of the pea plants in his garden generated 80% of the healthy pea pods.

This observation caused him to explore uneven distribution. He discovered that 80% of the land in Italy was owned by just 20% of the population. He investigated different industries and found that 80% of production typically came from just 20% of the companies. The generalization became the concept that 80% of results will come from 20% of the action.

While it does not always come to be an exact 80/20 ratio, this imbalance is often seen in various business cases:

- 20% of sales reps generate 80% of total sales
- 20% of customers account for 80% of total profits
- 20% of the most reported software bugs cause 80% of software crashes
- 20% of patients account for 80% of healthcare spending

RELATING THE 80/20 RULE TO HOUSE SELLING

Understanding the 80/20 rule concept can save you time in selling your house. Applying the 80/20 rule, you stop trying to sell people on the entire house. Applying the rule, you can highlight the 20% of your house's features that make it special. The remaining 80% of your house still affects the buyer's decision, so do not neglect it, but in photographs and showings, feature the elements that make your house special.

Your selling point won't be the common features your house shares with the other properties on the market. Instead, use your house's unique features to grab the attention of buyers who are interested in those distinctive features.

BUYER'S STORY

When Vince and Sue were shopping for a new house, Vince wanted an ocean view. They looked at many desirable properties but didn't find any that were right for them. Some were overpriced; others had obstructed views. The search went on for almost a year until they found an older house a short walk from the ocean.

The neglected exterior and dated interior were not encouraging, but when Vince stepped out onto the third-floor balcony off the master suite, he was sold. Any shortcomings in wall color or fixtures faded away when he took in the view. He could now see the sunrise from his bedroom window every morning.

What 20% of the house caught the eyes of Vince and Sue? The magnificent third-floor ocean view!

SELLER'S STORY

When Cam and Kate listed their house, they needed a buyer who wasn't concerned that the house was on an unpaved road. Though the house was over 10 years old, the interior was updated with fresh, neutral wall colors and carpeting to look brand new. The towering trees and established yard gave the house a welcoming appeal.

The buyers had also looked at a house within miles of Cam and Kate's that had towering trees as well as a koi pond and patio. This house was comparable in interior and exterior, but it was on a busy street.

What 20% of the house caught the buyer's eye and prompted him to choose Cam and Kate's house? The buyer loved the secluded country feel of the house. The 1.8-acre property was surrounded by pastures, with grand oaks dotting the landscape.

Sooo, instead of talking about everything that everyone else has, focus on what makes your house unique and special. Only one person will buy your house. The negatives may not matter to the "one buyer" who appreciates the 20% he or she is looking for.

LOCATION MATTERS

A buyer paid extra for a townhouse because of its location in the complex overlooking woods instead of the parking area. Another seller took advantage of the fact that most of the surrounding house s didn't have yards; only a few shared a half-acre grassy area. An owner whose townhouse bordered this yard area sold his house for a higher price than other townhouses in the complex on the market because his had a characteristic shared by fewer than 10% of others. He had the only available listing offering that feature. He pointed to that feature in marketing the townhouse. With this attractive point of difference, the house sold for a higher price.

Another townhouse seller in the same complex found a different unique feature. Although she did not have a yard, she was still able to use location to advantage. Her property backed up to a lake and fountain. This unique feature helped her to sell the townhouse quickly and for a better-than-average sales price.

THE 80/20 RULE IN ACTION: BUYERS ARE SEARCHING FOR UNIQUE FEATURES

Decide upon, improve, if necessary, and spotlight the unique features of your house in marketing copy, online and print photographs, and in showing the house. Do not spend much time explaining how the storage room can be converted to another full bath; instead, lead the dog-owning prospect to the fenced-off dog run in the unusually large backyard. If the house has a certain feature a buyer is specifically looking for, highlighting this aspect in marketing efforts will attract interested buyers willing to pay the asking price or better.

Each house will have its unique features. Here are some suggestions if you aren't sure of yours:

- Hilltop views or high vantage point, offering a spectacular view of the surrounding area
- Open fields frequented by wildlife
- Unobstructed views of sunrise and sunset
- Patios, decks, dog runs, garden areas, and gazebos — highlight items neighboring houses don't have, or differences in size or quality; that one vital feature could help you sell your house
- Location can set a property apart, even in the same area, adding value to a house in a cul-de-sac or on a corner lot
- A private location or lot partially concealed by trees
- A unique, shady, or larger backyard; a fenced backyard is a big selling point (if your yard can be fenced, but is not, consider making that improvement)
- Finished basement, large attic or garage, swimming pool, or anything else that makes your house stand out

LOOK FOR THE 20% DIFFERENCE AND MARKET THE FEATURE

Following the 80/20 rule can lessen time showing to people who are not interested. Instead, you will be showing your house to buyers who are motivated to make a purchase.

You won't have to show as frequently. You also won't have to sift through low-ball offers from casual shoppers. Keeping this in mind, you must take the time to uncover your house's most attractive and unique features and improve them to their highest potential. Compare your house with others in the neighborhood to see what makes yours stand out. Work with that what you have. I know we've spent a good deal of time on the 80/20 rule but if you don't get this concept, you will suffer for it.

HOW THE 80/20 RULE APPLIES TO HOUSE SALES

An out-of-town house shopper with no specific requirements contacted a real estate agent to look at available house s for sale. The agent drove him from house to house. In each case, the buyer suggested offers 10% to 20% below the asking price without budging. As the day progressed, the agent's chances of finding a suitable house were dwindling.

They stopped at one last house as the sun set. The exterior of the house was dated and the yard untended. This agent and her client had spent the entire day looking at houses that shared 80% of the same features.

Nevertheless, once the buyer walked into the room, he wanted to buy the house for asking price.

What set this house apart from the others? He wasn't too interested in the kitchen, bathrooms, and bedrooms. A bedroom was a bedroom as far as he was concerned. He fell in love with the one remarkable feature of this otherwise uninspiring house.

The house sat on a hill with a beautiful view out a large window. As they entered the great room, the sun was setting below the distant tree line. That view sold the buyer. The remaining parts of the house could be improved.

The house buyer based his decision to buy on the window view from the hillside. The "20%" of the house's features motivated him to offer full price on the spot. Such is the power of the 80/20 rule.

In some cases, the 80/20 rule may help people make a sale without even conducting a showing. The house in the following example had languished on the market for months. Unlike the previous house, this one was attractive. On the contrary, it was a brand-new, custom-built house. It sat on the market for over seven months without a single offer.

The builder hired a real estate agent who knew the importance of finding that one special feature. He drove out to give the house a thorough investigation. He discovered what the property had that the competition did not. The house had a five-acre yard. Other houses being sold in the area had one to two acre lots.

Not only was the yard bigger, but it was also more private than the other properties. The real estate agent marketed the property highlighting the five acres along with a description of the house. Because the house was no longer the main selling point, interest in the property increased.

That's it on the 80/20 concept:

1. Work with what you have
2. Improve it
3. Find what is unique about your property
4. Start packing (literally get rid of stuff)
5. Focus your marketing and showings on that rather than the other common features of every other house on the market.

3

Staging For Vision

Staging is the act of sprucing and setting up a house to make it as visually appealing as possible to a prospective buyer. Creating an eye-appealing house — one that potential buyers can envision themselves living in — is the best investment in the sales effort.

Sellers often fail to take full advantage in this regard, as it takes considerable time, expertise and money. However, the payoff is proven. Staging is considered one of the most effective marketing strategies to increase the value of your house.

This strategy is effective in any market, in any type of house or property being listed. It applies equally to single-family houses, apartments, townhouses, condos and farms. This approach works! Agents and sellers using this tactic have a greater chance of selling the property for more money.

** Hot Tip **

Don't penny pinch! If you worry about the 6% you might pay the Realtors and advertising, you are cheating yourself. Worry about your 94% you keep! Don't worry about the few dollars it may cost to Stage the house, worry about being competitive and more desirable than the other houses ~ get your house sold and get more money for your efforts! Believe me you are not the first; but now you know.

In today's competitive real estate market, selling your house requires hard work and dedication. A motivated seller can bring the house to the marketing forefront.

Staging the house will:

- Distinguish it from the competition
- Attract top dollar from house buyers
- Provide a visual edge over the competition

STAGING VS. NON-STAGED
CASE STUDY & REPORT

Dear Reader,

I wanted to give you the most convincing proof possible. Many people find it hard to believe that the simple act of staging helps one house sell for more than another, similar house.

In my research, I looked for examples of similar houses being sold for differing amounts of money where only one of the two houses was staged.

The clearest example I could find was in the case of these two listings. This development has 200 equivalent townhouses. Every single townhouse in the neighborhood is three stories with three bedrooms and three bathrooms. Every unit has the same floor plan. I looked for two sales there, and found these:

- Townhouse A sold on August 26.
- Townhouse B (5 doors down) sold on July 26, for 40,000 dollars less.

I visited this neighborhood, and I am familiar with these properties.

You could not find a better example of two identical properties that sold for different prices.

The details show these two houses are identical in every substantial way:

The lots the units sit on are identical as far as the desirableness of the location.

Both units had the same kitchen plan with the same cabinets and a tile floor.

Both units had nice hardwood floors in the living room and carpeted bedrooms.

Every important detail of these townhouses was identical. I studied every aspect of these sales to find what made the difference.

There are two reasons one house sold for $40,000 more than the other:

- Townhouse A was professionally staged, giving it a more appealing appearance.
- The agent selling Townhouse A took higher quality, more attractive photos of the house .

Those two seemingly small actions made the $40,000 difference! The buyers of Townhouse A made a higher offer because the agent presented the house in a more appealing and attractive way. *B Curry, Realtor. Used with the permission of the author.*

THE POWER OF STAGING
WHEN SELLING A HOUSE

Consider these results from surveys conducted by Coldwell Banker and the National Association of Realtors®:

- Staged houses spent 50% less time on the market than houses that were not staged.
- Staged houses sold for more than 6% above asking price.
- A staging investment of 1% to 3% of asking price generates an ROI of between 8% and 10%.
- Houses staged prior to listing sold 79% faster than houses staged after listing.

WHAT DO BUYERS WANT TO SEE?

Most house shoppers are envisioning a fresh start. If they can picture themselves living in the house, the house will be easier to sell. This is known as "interior curb appeal," where the eyes are drawn to inviting spaces and light, as well as to unique features. Each room needs a purpose or suggested use. The house must feel new to reflect ease of upkeep. The goal is to create a clean, simple, and contemporary feel. Painting, updating fixtures, and eliminating stained carpets and popcorn ceilings can affect the saleability of the house by 75%!

NEUTRALIZE FOR EYE APPEAL

The idea is to *neutralize* the house regarding personal taste or decoration such that buyers can easily envision the house as it would be outfitted in *their* taste or with *their* possessions - without the distractions of the seller's taste and possessions. In staging, distractions are removed so the house shopper can imagine living in each space of the house.

An effective way to achieve this is to paint all rooms in a neutral color. A wide range of neutrals from soft grays to warm beiges are available. Painting the interior gives newness and freshness and can make the house appear more spacious. Using the same color in visibly adjacent rooms gives the house a seamless look and uninterrupted flow.

Changing your window coverings to match the walls can create an illusion of more space. Dark or bold wall colors can dampen interest in a house if used in large spaces; however, they can be used effectively as accent colors.

FOCUS ON FURNITURE: LESS IS MORE

In staging, a visibly inviting space is created so that the house shopper can envision or imagine life in that space. Minimization is the key. If the seller's personal taste and style is showcased while the house is on the market, it may be a sale distraction. Preparing for moving is part and parcel of selling a house; it might as well be done at this stage of the process to enhance the property's saleability. Start packing and move it off site.

Shortly, we will examine depersonalizing the house, a key step. First, however, we must examine the concept of creating space by minimizing furniture.

Buyers are attracted to houses flooded with light and roominess. They are equally put off by cramped houses filled with un-navigable spaces. House shoppers want to walk through a house without obstacles in the way. Space and storage are high on the list of buyers' desires, so every area of the house should feel spacious. It's all psychological.

Remove all unnecessary furniture from living spaces. Store it while the house is marketed. Closets, pantries, and storage rooms must be free of clutter and look organized. Pruning back on what fills up space and relegating it to a storage unit creates interest by showcasing ample space and storage and not overflowing closets, garage and other areas.

Furniture placement is an easy way to highlight unique house features. A grouping of chairs in front of a fireplace will draw attention to it. Avoid pushing furniture close to the walls. Reposition easy chairs into floating group spaces.

Every room must be staged to show *function.* An empty room used for overflow of boxes, possessions, or unwanted items should be transformed into a usable, desirable space. Clean it out and create an office space with a desk and chair or a reading room with a lamp and recliner. Exercise equipment might be arranged to feature it as a workout room. Every room should have a purpose and be user-friendly. Make your house's traffic flow obvious so buyers can browse each room without effort or spatial trauma.

EMOTIONAL CUES

Once every room has a purpose, creating atmosphere is crucial to making the house desirable. Decorative touches of greenery, flowers, and lit candles give life to a room. Creatively hung wall art can do the same. A bedroom that has one bed with one pillow and blanket may make the room seem bare and lonely. By adding a table with decor and a rocking chair draped with a lap robe, you heighten its appeal. Be sure to add elements of the same color, shape, or texture to unify the room. Any splashes of bold color should appear in wall art or any place you want to draw attention.

If you can't move, learn to strike a balance between staging and living in your house. You can seasonally decorate your house without dashing your appeal. The main goal is to keep your house clean and free of clutter that distracts would-be buyers. Even simple things can make a big impact on the final sale price of a house. Staging done well is one of those things! You have two options for staging a house: do it yourself or hire a professional house stager. If you are considering hiring someone, we can provide recommendations.

TO STAY OR NOT TO STAY?

House sellers often ask whether they should stay in their house while it is on the market or go. There are pros and cons to both and factors that can tip the scale to one side.

If the seller has engaged a real estate agent, the burden of showing the house is virtually eliminated. The agent will field all calls, set appointments, and show the house. Relatedly, chances that a buyer's real estate agent will show your house are increased. Busy schedules often cause agents, as with anyone, to take the path of least resistance. If they have 20 houses to show and 5 are occupied, they may well show the vacant houses because it's easier. They don't have to call and make an appointment. They can simply go over and use the lockbox which records when, who and how long the agent was there.

Further, the continual pressure to keep daily life from affecting the house's pristine staging presentation isn't there. As a seller you are not under constant pressure to keep the house in immaculate showing condition and spotless. If you might be unwilling to keep the house in turnkey condition for showing purposes, consider vacating before putting the house on the market. There are situations in which it is almost essential to vacate the house during the selling period—e.g., if the sellers' house is simply too messy to show while the sellers live there.

Reasons for messy houses vary. Some sellers are pack-rats, and their house reflects that behavior because boxes are piled everywhere, and rooms are stuffed to the gills with personal belongings. This is a considerable obstacle to getting a good offer. Other sellers have several children, which can obviously present difficulty in always maintaining a clean, show-ready house.

Potential buyers should be alerted that the seller has vacated the house to best show it. Otherwise, a vacant house can be interpreted as meaning a "motivated seller" who needs to sell quickly. Often, with an empty house, sellers are motivated. One comment on a real estate on-line forum tells of making an offer of $30,000 less than the asking price, believing the owners might be getting desperate to sell. They were asking $300,000. The buyer was sold on it anyway and would have paid more, but "haggling" began well below what was expected because the buyer read the fact that the house was unlived in as a clue to a desperate-to-sell owner. Decide what is best for you and proceed.

4

Upgrading Not With Profit In Mind

Making upgrades can be as easy as replacing the handset on your front door or as daunting as remodeling a kitchen, bathroom or even repainting the entire house. The question is always what house improvements give the best return on the remodeling dollar?

Return on Investment (ROI) is generally less than 100% in real estate, so the rule of thumb is "less is more." It is frequently advised in this area that it's better to update/remodel your house while living in it and not solely at the time it comes to sell. That way, there is more enjoyment in the improvement and less cost in preparing for sale. Some desirable upgrades or house improvements will not return their cost in the sale price.

In 2016, back in the olden days, a remodeling publication said the best ROI improvement a house seller can make is insulating the attic space, with a 116% return. If your house is worth $275,000 and you spend $25,000 to revamp the kitchen, don't make the mistake of assuming that the investment will increase the value, dollar for dollar. The remodel may add value to the house, but the return in dollars spent will be around 50%. Smaller upgrades, like replacing outdated fixtures in the kitchen and bath, are certainly worthwhile, but major remodeling of those rooms is not wise, just to sell your house.

That's not to say you can ignore necessary repairs that a house inspector would red-flag or mortgage company would demand before issuing a loan to a buyer. If major problems, like a leaking roof or outdated electrical wiring, exist, you may want to repair those before putting your house on the market, or expect to give concessions to the buyer.

STARTING WITH THE BASICS

Every listed house should meet the basic expectations of any buyer; it should have a sound roof, functioning gutters and downspouts, foundation without cracks, functioning heating and/or air-conditioning system, solid subflooring, and safe and secure electrical wiring. Bank mandated house inspections will require most shortcomings to be required to be remedied to get buyer financing approval. It is better to fix the issues prior to putting on the market. You want to eliminate objections and sell for a higher price.

It is important to understand that the market value of a house is largely determined by the prices of comparable houses recently sold in the area. Extensive remodeling to sell the house or to increase the value may not pay off. The property needs to be up to the standards of neighboring houses, so while the kitchen needs to be comparable to others, as in the example above, spending $25,000 to remodel a kitchen in an area where comparable houses recently sold for $275,000 will not increase the house's value to $300,000. While it may be a helpful selling feature, it won't return dollar-for-dollar value, in this case.

MECHANICAL MAINTENANCE IS A MUST

It is easy to get wrapped up in the more eye-pleasing aspects of preparing a house to sell. However, the up-keep of the more mundane aspects of the house cannot be overlooked.

These mechanical features require consideration:

· Electrical boxes and wiring
· Natural gas lines
· Plumbing

- Central heating and air-conditioning
- Garage and inside doors of all types

If these components are old, outdated, or not working correctly, the house's appeal is lowered, as is the eventual sale price. Again, ideally these should be working while you live in and enjoy the house.

According to the National Association of Realtors®, 65% of house buyers surveyed wanted to be sure their new house had a working central air system. Of the 31 mechanical features inquired about in the survey, this was the most important.

People want to purchase a house that reflects their aesthetic tastes and lifestyles, but also one that is safe and sound. Faulty electrical systems do not provide a feeling of safety. Leaky plumbing arouses concerns of mold infestation, sewage problems and future unknown expenses. These areas can require extensive work and they are extremely important. Overlook them in the preparation stage and you run the risk of trouble and a cancelled Escrow later when inspections and appraisals are done.

It aids the sale if professionals certify or remediate any deficiencies in the mechanical systems. Having a professional inspection for buyers to review is a big plus in marketing.

- Have a certified plumber inspect the entire water system for leaks. Check the well and septic field, if applicable.
- Hire an electrician to check the wiring.
- Call an HVAC company and have technicians perform a thorough service checkup.
- Contact the natural gas supplier and have them double-check the mechanics of your tank and lines.

If you're looking for an alternative to calling and arranging all the different inspections, certified house inspectors usually cover all items related to mechanical issues (and more). They will be able to identify possible trouble spots. Many buyers hire an inspector, so you may be saving them a major step in the sale process and removing fatal objections.

If you have mechanical issues and decide to sell your house "as is," it may be necessary to negotiate with the buyer.

REPLACING APPLIANCES

New appliances undoubtedly make an impact on buyers. The National Association of Realtors® conducted a survey of buyers and found that:

- Buyers were usually "interested" or "somewhat interested" in buying a house that featured new appliances
- Roughly 17% of respondents preferred stainless steel
- The most important factor: available appliances
- Most buyers who were unable to get their sought-after appliances said they would have been willing to pay, on average, nearly $2,000 more for them.

Potential buyers want appliances included and will pay more for them, especially if they are new or in excellent condition. New appliances might be what sets a house apart from the house for sale across the street. If new appliances are out of reach, offer immaculately clean and fully functioning existing ones.

UPDATING HARDWARE

Carefully inspect your bathroom and kitchen hardware. If it is unsightly or worn, it's best to replace it. Put yourself in a buyer's shoes. Your house will potentially be their new home. Old, worn-out fixtures are not going to speak to them the way nice, new shiny hardware will.

Unless your knobs, pulls, handles, or hinges are broken, you need not replace them. Get that fresh look simply by thoroughly washing, sanding, and painting them with spray paint made specifically for kitchen and bath hardware, making it cost-effective. Consider though, it could be faster and simpler to replace them. You get to decide.

Check these hardware items closely and replace, as needed:

- Towel bars
- Toilet paper holder
- Door handles
- Dated light fixtures

The goal is to touch up your house nicely without excessive spending. The Internet and YouTube University has a wealth of do-it-yourself videos that can help you update your bath and kitchen if your budget is limited.

If you have broken or worn-out hardware, it is best to replace the entire set. If you can find matching pieces, you can paint the old and new to match.

LET THERE BE LIGHT

Whether natural or artificial, bringing in light is one of the most effective ways to show off your house.

Using light to enhance your house's appeal can make a difference. Harsh light is unflattering, even to the best furnishings and features. Dim lighting gives everything in the house a dingy feel. Assessing the lighting in each area of your house will give you a quick idea where to bring in more light. Rooms with abundant windows greatly benefit from natural light, as your house will be seen during the day.

Supplemental light is necessary for rooms with smaller windows or little natural light coming in. Increase the wattage of light bulbs in your lamps to improve artificial light. As a rule of thumb, there should be 100 watts for each 50 square feet of space.

There are three kinds of lighting. General lighting or overhead is typically ambient. The pendant light is good for tasks like food preparation or reading. Accent lights are usually on tables or mounted on walls. You can use all three to bring out the best your house has to offer.

Key areas, such as foyers, can set the stage by impressing buyers with a dramatic light source. If you do not have an abundance of natural light coming in, a chandelier-type light works if your ceilings are high. Otherwise, wall sconces are impressive in smaller spaces. Do not assume you need to buy new fixtures if you can update existing ones. The aim is to make sure each area of the house is effectively lit.

Kitchen and bathrooms are pivotal rooms. These two areas can make or break a sale. The combination of ambient, natural, and pendant light can bring out the best in your kitchen space. Mounting track lighting underneath cabinets gives the counters a chance to shine aesthetically and functionally. Make sure the light over the sink area is sufficient and working properly. If you have a hood over the stove, install clear bulbs to ensure the brightest light

Lighting in the bathroom needs to be intense without being harsh. Soft lighting enhances any part of the house you want to highlight.

Avoid harsh lighting in the bedrooms, as well. Lamps strategically placed will give the bedrooms a peaceful, restful feel although the closet light should be bright and plentiful.

One last tip: Lightly painted rooms still need sufficient light so the room does not appear drab.

FLOORING PLAN

Although you want to avoid house shoppers looking down on your house, they will be looking down at *what is under their feet*. Your house's value can be downgraded by the buyer if your floors are in bad shape. On the flip side, if your house's flooring is well done and in excellent condition, buyers will be more willing to pay more for it.

Maximizing profit without compromising investment dollars is the goal, but if flooring and carpeting are not in salable shape, you need to take inventory. There is no point in spending money unnecessarily if the improvements do not add significant value or help the house sell quickly; however, there are options that don't break the budget.

Repairing and thoroughly cleaning the floors are the least expensive way. Take stock by examining all floors. Move furniture out of the way and make notes regarding condition, stains, or blemishes. Write down what needs to be replaced, cleaned, or repaired.

Carpets can be steam cleaned to eliminate stains and odors. If the carpets are path-worn and dull, you can replace them easily with other kinds of flooring with a reasonable ROI, although carpeting does make a room, especially a bedroom, feel cozy. Laminate floors can be cosmetically fixed with repair kits found at house improvement stores.

Hardwood flooring can be easily refinished if the wood is worn or water damaged. Seek the advice of a flooring professional because real wood floors add a level of quality to a house that laminate or vinyl floors cannot match. By the way, the difference in Laminate and Vinyl is simple. Laminate is a thin layer of actual wood on top of generally the same material as would be with the Vinyl flooring. It is important to note because Vinyl is thought to be water proof while Laminate is thought to be water resistant. If water sits on Laminate (wood) for a long period of time, it will damage it where Vinyl will survive and not absorb. Both are durable materials with a little padding on the bottom that will dampen or remove the hollow sound you could get walking on wood.

TIPS FOR KITCHEN AND BATH

When making upgrades to kitchen and bath, keep in mind of what constitutes a substantial investment. The key is to consider the mass appeal for the sake of re-sale value. One house owner decided to add a backsplash and more cabinet space in the kitchen and then updated the appliances and refinished the oak flooring. Total cost was $4,000. The seller kept the price comparable to sales in the area and ending up selling for $27,000 more than the asking price because interested buyers started a bidding war!

You do not need to bust your budget to sell your house, but you do want to have mass appeal. Kitchens are a pivotal area in house appeal.

Here are some suggestions of what you can do to your kitchen and bath to impress buyers without losing ROI:

- Paint neutral colors.
- Add a new backsplash in kitchen.
- Install new countertops if dated or below current area standards.
- Add new, multi-functional kitchen faucets to add mass appeal.
- Add cabinet space or increase storage in the pantry.
- Replace dated bathroom vanities. Pedestal sinks or trendy cabinet sinks have mass appeal.
- Replace toilet seats and bath/shower handles and faucets

TWO ENERGY-SAVING UPGRADES TO LOWER UTILITY BILLS

- Install an energy-saving smart thermostat (less than $300) that saves on utility bills.
- Install solar vents ($500-$700) in the attic space that help expel hot air during summer months.

MAKING A CASE FOR SPACE

When people accumulate an abundance of posses-sions, they need space to store it. They also want a way to clear the clutter. According to the National Association of Realtors®, most house buyers would have preferred improved and greater closet space, as well as other storage options. Consider these statistics showing what buyers are looking for in a house :

- 93% wanted a laundry room
- 90% wanted a bathroom linen closet
- 86% wanted garage storage
- 85% wanted a walk-in kitchen pantry

STORAGE IS A PLUS

Give buyers great storage and you've won their hearts. If you can add new closets to your house easily, do so. Building a simple closet is not difficult if you are moderately handy. If you're selling an older house, where closet space is typically minimal, this will help! If your rooms are already small, you might not want to take any square footage away from them. Existing closets can be updated with shelving to maximize the space at hand.

If you don't have the skills or the funds to hire someone to build new space, consider investing in closet organizers to make the most of what space you have. For instance:

- You can easily design your custom closet kit online with a storage solution company like Closet Maid.

- Your standard superstore or hardware store often has exactly what you need in an inexpensive, pre-fabricated form.
- Organizers won't enlarge your closets but maximizing vertical and horizontal space is a suitable alternative.

And don't stop there — after all, storage isn't restricted to closets. Storage improvement opportunities apply to all cabinets, clothes closets, linen closets, and attic and basement spaces.

Make sure you organize your cabinets. The same retailers that provide closet organizers can help with this. Take a good look at your laundry room and linen closet. Adding extra shelving in these places can make a big impact.

Look for any place you can provide attractive and inexpensive storage space. Make sure your improvements are tasteful, and you will benefit from increased storage solutions.

Updating your house with ROI in mind is the best approach in the decision-making process when preparing your house to be ready to sell. Look over this recent list of what buyers want in a house. Compare it to what you have in yours, and upgrade accordingly without surpassing the price line for comparable houses in your area.

FEATURES MOST HOUSE BUYERS WANT

- Energy Star-rated appliances — 94%
- Laundry room — 93%
- Energy Star rating for the whole house — 91%
- Exhaust fan in bathroom — 90%
- Exterior lighting — 90%
- Energy Star-rated windows — 89%
- Ceiling fans — 88%
- Garage storage — 86%
- Table space for eating in kitchen — 85%
- Walk-in kitchen pantry — 85%

Keep in mind these features are not guaranteed to be effective or profitable upgrades but they will help you compete.

FEATURES FEWER BUYERS WANT

- Shower stall without a tub in the master bath — 51%
- Second story family room — 43%
- Wet bar — 41%
- Laminate countertop — 40%
- Outdoor kitchen or Game room — 31%
- His & her baths — 31%
- Glass-front cabinets — 31%

5

The Three D's

DEPERSONALIZED

Staging is readying the house to show to potential buyers; you must encourage buyers to visualize living in the house itself, but *not in your* house.

Depersonalizing the house involves removing your personal items, such as photos, trophies, and collectibles. Knickknacks and wall decor are also personal taste items that may distract buyers from seeing the house as theirs. It is not personal, but no one — besides you — will appreciate your beer can collection, antique kitchen accessories, overstuffed closets, VHS/CD/DVD/records collections, and general clutter, except you. Simplify and neutralize your house as if it were a model house, because that is exactly what it is while it's on the market.

It's not personal, but no one — besides you — will appreciate your beer can collection, antique kitchen accessories, overstuffed closets, VHS/CD/ records collections, and general clutter, except you. Simplify and neutralize your house as if it were a model house, because that is exactly what it is while it's on the market. (No, not an error, this was repeated for emphasis, it's that important - It must be done!)

Pack and store your treasured items out of sight. Consider monthly rented storage units until your house sells. Anything is possible, and you don't want something valuable to disappear. Consider removing valuables as well as prescription medication. Yes, thieves do shop open houses.

Make your house a clean, welcoming, blank canvas upon which any buyer can visually paint their own dreams. It will not feel like your house during the showing period, but once you sell and move into your next place, you can decorate that house any way you like.

DE-CLUTTER AND DISCARD

It is understandably inconvenient to live in your house without your "stuff," like living in a hotel. However, it is a necessary component of getting top dollar for your house.

Extra furniture and items like books, magazines, CD collections, and hobby supplies add weight and visual distraction in a room. Your salt & pepper shaker collection is going to look like clutter, even if the buyer collects salt & pepper shakers. The more spacious your house appears, the more appealing it will be. Minimize as much as possible. You want the house shopper to see what your house has to offer, not to guess about the potential or possibilities; as a bonus, you'll be ½ packed when it's time to move.

Work From A Plan

List each room of the house, noting the clutter in each room, including closets.

- De-clutter rooms one at a time, attacking from the largest project to the smallest
- Clear out each room, keeping only essential item
- Donate or discard clothes, decor, toys, and other items no longer used
- Box up possessions you want to keep but do not currently use; put them in storage
- Keep surfaces clean and free of collected items

Room-by-Room List:

- **Kitchen** — Clear the counters, leaving only three or four essential items. Keep towels, dishrags, and potholders out of sight. Soaps and cleaners should be stored under the sink. Rarely used small appliances can be packed and put in storage. Pack away teacups, serving dishes, and platters if you normally showcase them. If you want to draw attention to decorative shelving, put a few pieces out for show. Seasonal dishes and accessories should also be stored. Remove any pest control traps or poison from the pantry and closets. Appliances are not extra shelving or storage. Buyers will not want to find the microwave used as a bread box or the oven as cookware storage.

- **Bathrooms** — Make the bathroom look as though it's rarely used. Remove everything from the cabinets and drawers. Keep what you need or will use and discard the rest. Store prescription medications out of sight and out of reach. Find a safe place for jewelry, keepsakes, and cosmetics/perfumes. Store hair products and styling tools in the cabinets.

- **Bedrooms** — When it comes to clothing, people generally wear 20% of the clothes they own, 80% of the time. The focus is showcasing closet space. Only hang clothes that you wear most often and store the rest.

- **Dining Areas** — Clear clutter off any flat surfaces, including the dining table, leaving only subtle decor such as a vase of flowers.

- **Living Areas** (living rooms, family rooms, and great rooms) — Gather stacks of books, magazines, remotes, toys, and gaming gadgets, and throws. Again, clear all flat surfaces, packing away nonessential items and store electronics in decorative bins. Fold and drape throws on chairs.

- **Office Space** — Organization is the focus for office space. Overflowing shelves do not reflect useful space. Keep all personal papers stored out of sight.
- **Linen Closets** — Organize and clean out. Store seasonal blankets, clothes, and outerwear off site. Keep linens to a minimum.
- **Laundry Room** — Whether your washer and dryer are in the basement, laundry room, or closet, you should make the room or area neat. Organize what you keep with shelving or bins. Don't leave clothes on the floor. Store detergents, bleach, and softeners in cabinets. Do not use the tops of the appliances for storage.
- **Garage** — Although cleaning the garage may be the most daunting of de-cluttering tasks, it can be as simple as getting rid of things you haven't touched in years. Boxes of broken toys, useless sports gear, and rusty tools all seem to migrate to the dark corners of the garage. Use this opportunity to donate or discard. Other items like wall paint, extra tiles for the floor, and bicycles can be shelved or hung.
- **Pets** — Pet items also need to be out of the way when a buyer comes by. See the section on Pet Peeves on how to deal with pets while selling your house.

DEEP CLEANING: SPOTLESS IS THE NAME OF THE GAME

Doing a thorough, deep cleaning of your house is vital. It works for people selling a car (they get more money), and it will work for you when selling your house (you get more money). With the house depersonalized and de-cluttered, it might make sense to use a professional deep-cleaning residential service.

Otherwise, with the clutter gone, move on to cleaning each room. Tidy each room from top to bottom. Be meticulous, especially in the kitchen, bathrooms and window blinds. House buyers will open cabinets, pantries, and closets to assess their storage needs.

GENERAL LIST OF TO-DOS:

- Clear the cobwebs from every corner of your house
- Dust ceiling fans and lighting fixtures
- Dust and clean the blinds
- Wash the walls. This has to be done before repainting, so this will save you time later.
- Clean all glass surfaces: mirrors, television screens, patio doors, and tables.
- Polish all wooden surfaces
- Wipe down leather furniture

- Clean out and reorganize kitchen cabinets. Buyers will open them.
- Attack all appliances with cleaning fervor. Make them shine!
- Scrub sinks, toilets, tubs, showers, faucets, and countertops. They must be impeccable.
- All tiled areas, including grout, must be free of discoloration, stains, and mildew.
- Clean the window treatments. Wash the windows so that the natural light will enhance your living space.
- Vacuum rugs, shampoo carpets, and mop floors thoroughly

KITCHEN AND BATH: FOCUS ON HIGH-IMPACT AREAS

The most important rooms in your house are the kitchen and bathrooms. A kitchen can sell a house because it is the heart of a house, the place family and friends gather to enjoy one another's company. Buyers will be turned off by dirt and grime, cooking smells, and trash. Clean all cabinet surfaces as well as under the sink.

Bathrooms are so important to Americans that most houses have at least two or three. As you work toward selling your house, it is imperative that the bathrooms are kept clean and odor-free. Potential buyers might forgive a less-than-stellar child's room, but a questionable bathroom or kitchen could cost you a sale.

PET PEEVES

Pets are wonderful, but house buyers want to see your house without them. Domestic animals are not unique features or selling points of houses; pet dander and odor aren't going to provide a positive viewing experience. Some prospects might have allergies, others may not like animals, and for all, they are an unnecessary distraction. Minimize the presence of pets. Dog dishes, cat litter boxes, and beds need to be clean. Pets should be relegated to cages or backyards while showing your house. With all the staging work complete, you are now ready to list and showcase your house.

In the next section, you will learn how to price your house. An experienced real estate professional is your best information source for how to sell your house quickly without lowering the price. When selling your house, there is much to know about pricing, marketing, and negotiations.

6

How To Market
Your "House"

The purpose of this book is to provide insight and guidance on how to sell a house quickly and for more money. Previous chapters concerned real estate sales terminology and concepts, with a heavy emphasis on the dos-and-don'ts of getting a house listing ready for the most effective presentation, and thus price. The goal of upcoming chapters is to help in understanding what determines price and market value of a house — specifically, *your* house.

Despite the term "buyer's market," understand that it's always a "seller's market," too, in that houses are necessary and house ownership is cherished in the United States. We do not live in caves or nomadic tents. Real estate is a commodity that will remain so.

Further, your house is unique. There is no other exactly like it. Whatever individuality you have created on your property makes it stand apart from your neighbors' house.

There are no set rules of when to sell, because houses are not sold from store shelves based on seasonal holidays. People get new jobs or are transferred or decide to move because of family situations all the time, at any time of year.

Your house's value will be based on the sale price of similar houses purchased recently at the time you decide to sell, regardless of season. The bottom line is that you decide the asking price of your house either by yourself or with the help of a real estate professional.

How do you decide? What is the best way to get online exposure? Do professional photographs make a difference to online shoppers? What more can be done to market your house? Upcoming chapters answer these questions to help you sell your house for the best possible price.

THE PRICE IS RIGHT

A buyer of real estate is no different from a buyer of a painting or a bag of oranges. Both sellers' and buyers' perception of value will always have a prominent role during the sale. Perceived value and market value are not the same.

You need to know how to price your house strategically and correctly from the get-go to obtain the best price. A Virginia realty agency reported that houses in August of a certain year, sold for an average of 2.08% above list price within their first week on the market. Houses that grew stale for months sold for an average of 11.53% below the original list price.

As a seller, keep in the forefront of your mind two things as you determine initial listing price. First, sentimentality has no dollar value. Although you have emotional connections to your house, the buyer does not. Most buyers being shown many properties do not expect yours to be "the one." You will have to work to get them to that decision. Avoid letting sentiment play a part in pricing the property. Set all emotions aside during the selling process. Buyers look for cues to figure out your motivation to sell.

Next, there is also no direct dollar-for-dollar correlation between upgrade investment and market price. A $25,000 kitchen renovation will not necessarily bring the market price of a $675,000 to $700,000; don't assume you can add that amount to your asking price and get trapped by making your house the nicest, but also priciest, house for your area.

SALE PRICE VS. MARKET VALUE

If you have a ready-to-buy, bank-qualified buyer who is willing to pay a price you will accept, that is referred to as "sale price." It is an objective fact without influence.

This sale price transaction, once complete, will influence the market value of houses in the area. You determine the price of your house by looking at comparable local sales provided by a professional real estate agent, your property's condition, and the current supply and demand.

What a piece of property might sell for based on features and benefits in a competitive market, and the current supply and demand of similar houses is its *market value.* You might value your house at a higher price than what a buyer will pay or its true market price. Balanced markets will equalize market price and market value.

The perspectives of buyers and sellers also come into play when placing value on a house. Let's say your house has an abundance of mature trees — a plus in your mind. But a buyer who loathes raking leaves will see that as a negative.

If you just spent $10,000 to replace your roof, you might think you can set a higher price, but buyers already expect the roof to be in excellent shape. Proximities to schools, bus routes, and medical facilities can also create value that certain buyers are willing to pay for.

Buyers look for the right deal, but what they are willing to pay or the bank is willing to finance always has limits. Strategic pricing is your greatest tool when selling your house.

PRICING EXAMPLE

A house owner decides to place his house on the market and must decide on an asking price. By rough estimate, the house's market value falls between $990,000 and $1,200,000 of other houses currently on the market.

*** Secret ***

Remember the "price listed" is arbitrary. The Buyer will make an offer of some amount for reasons we likely don't know, then you negotiate from there. Make sure they can find your house online because that's where their search will start.

These are some pricing considerations and approaches to finding that "right price":

- **The "leave room for negotiation" approach.** In this approach, the market value is "stretched," say to $1,305,000. The price will not entice a buyer, but may make comparable houses seem more desirable. The house will most likely not sell quickly or at that price.

- **The "price it according to "worth" approach.** This approach sees the price set right between the market value benchmarks, at $1,105,000. Likely, house shoppers will lump the house with like-priced houses, knowing they can buy it anytime for $1,105,000.
- **The "underpricing generates interest" approach.** Underpricing at $950,000 will motivate buyers and perhaps create a bidding war. But the goal of selling the house for more money can be derailed. It's a good strategy but you might come up short.

THE COMPETITIVE MARKET ANALYSIS

When it comes to finding a buyer, pricing your house based on comparable real-priced sales is crucial to making the sale. The Comparative Market Analysis is imperative to pricing strategically. When you ask for a CMA from a real estate professional, be sure to review the analysis, ask questions, and get explanations. If completed correctly, this comparison report not only gives you a great listing price but also reduces the chance of your house being under-appraised. If you have a well-priced house, you should be showing within the first few days on the market. Offers should come within one week.

PERCEIVED VALUE

If the perceived value of your house by a potential buyer is greater than the actual price, the more willing he is to buy. The *urgency* to buy disappears the closer the price and perceived value are. This means marketing the house to match the buyer's specific needs and desires. A real estate agent can help you know the buyer's hot buttons, such that marketing and presentation can be tailored accordingly.

SELLING BY SHOWING OFF

Long ago, before the Internet, cell phones, and social media, buyers looking at houses perused the local Multiple Listing Service (MLS) book filled with tiny, grainy images of houses. Photos of featured houses (paid-for ads) were larger and sometimes in color, but most were black-

and-white, amateurish photos. The photo was insignificant compared to the information provided below it.

Today, the reverse is true. Photographs have become the most effective bait to attract a Realtor and internet searching buyers.

Getting your house sold quickly attracts future house owners. Recent studies show that 89% of buyers use online tools to shop for houses before contacting a real estate agent. They peruse the web, finding houses that appeal to them. Beautiful, engaging, photos of houses, inside and out make the best first impression. Online marketing through photographs is one of the most important ways to market your house.

Listing photography is a great tool for showing off the best features of your house. Bright and colorful shots of welcoming spaces encourage buyers to imagine themselves comfortable and living happily in your house. By focusing on the unique aspects of your house, like large rooms with great views or amazing architectural features, you can generate genuine interest. Stage your house to give the appearance of space and light in every photo without distorting reality.

*** Secret ***

Skip photos of most bath and bedrooms. If it's "just 4 walls," it may hurt more than help. A few special photos are better than 30 that don't help. The idea is to give buyers a reason to want to come see your house, not the opposite.

MAXIMUM TARGETED EXPOSURE

When you hire an agent, they can place your listing on all major real estate portals such as Zillow and Realtor.com. Buyers flock to these websites to find new listings they get from the MLS. The agent can also place your house on their own dedicated website and their social media outlets. In the average month, Zillow alone captures 69% of traffic to real estate websites. When you choose an agent to sell your house, make sure they offer the maximum targeted exposure to potential buyers through the online marketplace. Check to see if they are current with all techniques for online marketing and can provide the advanced technical services to sell your house:

- Visual maps such as Google Earth
- Floor plans or 3-D floor plans
- Video tours
- Updates on buyer activity through the agency
- Electronic documents
- Agency mobile device app

- Social media exposure
- Virtual house staging (if your house is empty)

Selling a house quickly and for more money takes work. Ensure the house is properly staged and ready to sell. Take advantage of every tool to achieve results. Work with a real estate agent who not only knows the value of good photography but who can also provide an aggressive internet marketing campaign to bring ready buyers to your listing.

7

Common Seller Mistakes

This list of frequent sellers' mistakes regarding house listing pricing can help you avoid the pitfalls involved in selling your house.

If setting a price was simple and straightforward, you would not need assistance in pricing your house correctly. Save yourself time and money by avoiding these costly mistakes.

PRICING MISTAKES

The first several seller mistakes you can avoid will save you thousands of dollars and involve the issue of *pricing*.

Guessing vs Researching

Basing your house price on what the neighbor down the street listed his house for isn't a reliable method. Nothing loses potential buyers faster than an overpriced house; and once they are gone, they are likely not to return. Subsequent price lowering makes it look like you're getting desperate to sell, which will increase low-ball offers. Contrarily, you do not want to under-price. A lower listing price may decrease the time to sell a bit; however, you might leave several thousand dollars on the table. Learn how to price your house for sale the right way, based on research.

The Comparative Market Analysis (CMA) is your best source for setting an asking price. If a house in your area sells for a low price, don't assume yours is worth the same amount. That house may have been a For Sale By Owner or have had condition issues or a personal issue requiring a very swift sale. Your house might have something to offer that the other one did not. Let the CMA be your guide with the advice of a real estate professional.

Hiring a Realtor from Highest-Price Suggestion

Choosing a real estate agent simply because they suggested a highest listing price for your house than other agents have suggested, is not in your best interest. A good Realtor will know more about the market for your house than you do. Pick an agent who can provide you with real numbers and solid marketing plans for your house. The person you choose to sell your house should be knowledgeable in the local area, trustworthy, and quick to answer questions or concerns regarding the entire selling process. Avoid this mistake by interviewing local agents (not just friends) and selecting the one who offers sales data and a strategic listing price, and not the highest price.

Subjective Pricing

Selling your house is a business transaction between a qualified buyer and yourself. If you have enjoyed living in your house for years, but have decided to move on, then don't let emotional attachments to the house affect how you price it. The most objective price will come from the CMA provided by your real estate agent. Memorable moments spent in your house are priceless, but they do not add to the selling price. It is also unrealistic to add dollars because of the labor spent making the house into your home which is now just a house again. By focusing on the CMA results and maintaining a firm strictly business attitude, you can keep emotions at bay.

First Day High-Price Blues

The most crucial time for your house is the first 10 days on the market. Once your house is on the MLS, you will see how much interest is generated. If your price is too high, buyers will pass you by because the house is out of their price range or out of kilter in the market area. By the time you decide to lower the price, they have moved on to other properties. As your house sits on the market, buyers will wonder why the house has not sold and conclude that it's undesirable in some way.

Price it correctly from the start to generate interest and gain attention from buyers to sell faster. Unrealistic pricing costs money in the long run. Which would you prefer to be? 1) The person who proudly proclaims their house is for sale for $xx.xx! or, 2) the person whose house already sold and they are moving on with their lives.

Un-rushed High Pricing

Even if you're not in a hurry to sell, it's not a wise move to test the market by listing your house at a high price to "see how it goes." Serious house shoppers may take months to find a new house. They are continually looking for new listings, not ones that have been sitting on the market. Thinking that the market will turn in your favor may not be reliable, either. If prices in your area are dropping, you may lose money. By pricing your house based on current market values, you can sell your house more quickly and for more money. Also, the MLS system now notes if a house was listed - then taken off the market - and listed again. It's an old trick that doesn't work anymore; everyone will know.

Price Dropping

Another pricing trap to avoid is listing a price for your house far above other houses in the area with the thought the price can be dropped if it does not sell after three months.

That is potentially workable in a stable or increasing market. However, if the market in your area is declining, you may be forced to reduce the price even more to catch up to the falling market. Price competitively from the beginning.

Do not hesitate to re-evaluate your local market. Work with your real estate agent to determine the fair market value of your house then market forces will create equilibrium to actual value.

OTHER SELLERS' MISTAKES

Zillow has compiled a list of "don'ts" to help people avoid the pitfalls of an otherwise successful sale.

Selling Before Getting Qualified Yourself

Entering a contract to sell your house before you get qualified to buy another is problematic. Your financial situation may have shifted since your last purchase, and you may not meet the requirements for a loan, or you may not be able to sell at a price that enables you to buy the kind of replacement house you desire. You might have to rent or buy another house that is far from ideal.

Before you decide to sell the house, get pre-approved by a lender you have confidence in and study the housing market in the area that you want to live to get a good idea how much it will realistically cost you to buy a replacement house. Make plans in case you must move right away.

Wasting Time on Unqualified Buyers

It is wasted effort to show your house to someone who cannot buy it. An example is the seller who spent two weeks preparing his house for an acquaintance who wanted to buy his house. The seller spent $4,000 removing an old shed and met with the prospect several times to discuss price and terms. It was well into the process when the seller found out the prospect (or current tenants) who could not qualify for a loan. Real estate agents spend considerable effort weeding out showings to non-qualified and unqualified house shoppers. If they can't or won't qualify the first week, move on and don't show.

Hovering

Whenever possible, don't be at home during a showing. This is impossible or impractical if you are selling the house yourself. If you have a real estate agent, leave before the house will be shown.

Lurking sellers make buyers nervous. Buyers may feel they are intruding and then rush through. They may be hesitant to talk about changes to the house or features they don't like. Buyers will feel uncomfortable thoroughly inspecting the house in the presence of the owners. It's easier for buyers to visualize the house being theirs when they have a chance to critique and discuss the house among themselves. If you must be home, try to stay out of the way, go outside, take a walk and answer few questions, only if asked.

** Hot Tip **

Buyers are not your friend. Smart buyers will try to get valuable information from a Seller in order to make their best, lowest offer. Don't be tricked into this situation; leave.

Unless there is a real reason for it, don't ask your agent to be present for all showings, either. That will limit your showing activity. Other agents want privacy with their buyers and they do not usually have time to work around your agent's schedule. An agent will use the lockbox which records who they are and how long they were in the house. It then relays that information to your agent to follow up. The system works, let it.

Waiting It Out

If you decide to wait, you are joining the thousands of other house owners who have also decided to wait. When a few decide it's time to take the plunge, you're already too late. If you need/want to sell now, then sell now. There will never be a better time.

Not Taking the First Quick Bid

This happens repeatedly. The seller gets a bite early on and is suddenly filled with confidence and pride that the house will easily sell and maybe even get involved in a bidding war. It feels like you're standing over a pond packed with a hungry fish. The first offer doesn't seem great and you naturally assume there must be bigger, juicier fish to be had. So, you throw the not-so-small-after-all fish back in. Big mistake. That "tiddler" is often the "catch of the day."

Becoming Friends with the Buyer

It's appropriate, even important, to be friendly, but don't let the personal nature of someone being in your house allow you to get into too many long discussions with the buyers, because personality conflicts often cloud judgments. Watch what is said in discussing items related to the house and neighborhood. Remember, this could be their new house. You're no doubt excited about moving. But buyers will start second guessing. A casual statement about the house "really being too small for a growing family," or "Make America Great Again", or "the schools are going through some changes" might be enough innocent chatter to squash their interest.

Underestimating Closing Costs

Many sellers only consider the money they are selling their house for. They don't appropriately calculate all the costs associated with the sale. Zillow lays out the following list of expenses:

- Real estate commission, if you use an agency to sell
- Advertising costs, signs, other fees, if you plan to sell by owner
- Attorney, closing agent, Escrow, local government and other professional fees
- Excise/Gains tax for the sale, if applicable
- Prorated costs for your share of annual expenses, such as property taxes, house owner association fees, and utilities
- Any other fees sometimes paid by the seller (appraisals, inspections, buyer's closing costs, etc.)

Spending Earnest Money Given to You

Do not believe that earnest money given at the time an offer is accepted is yours until the deal has closed and recorded. There are too many stories about sellers who spent the deposit money prior to closing. When the transactions did not occur for reasons such as financing contingency or failure of inspection or repair issues, the buyers had to fight or sue for a refund; and will win. Another advantage to using a real estate agent is to ensure a credible escrow company is a neutral party who will hold the deposit for you until closing day, and make sure your contract dictates what happens to the funds if the transaction doesn't close.

Forgetting to Cancel/Switch Utilities and Insurance

Many sellers overlook notifying utilities that they are moving or applying for utility service at their new house. Call the utilities and your insurance company as soon as a contract is signed. Find out how many days' lead time they need to switch or cancel, then get back with them when you have a firm closing date. This is not a big deal but it is something that happens too often and will cause you grief and a little extra costs if you forget.

Letting Emotions Take Over

Keep calm throughout the selling process, especially during and after a house inspection. Be practical and presume that issues will arise. It's not uncommon to have to pay for some repairs. If you really don't want to do the repair, offer a credit and let them do the repair themselves. Don't let the buyer's demand to complete a minor repair kill the deal.

On the other hand, don't commit to fixing anything in advance (e.g., "Sure, we can put on a new roof"), unless you are sure you can manage it emotionally and financially. Determine the kind of repairs you can practically take care of, then commit to that decision. Some repairs can become unmanageable and could cost you big money.

8

Learn From Other's Mistakes

To avoid selling your house for less than it's worth and leaving money on the table, it's helpful to find out what other people have done wrong. These are examples of costly mistakes, including mistakes made by banks.

No one is perfect and anyone can make mistakes. Remember when you saw your friend go through drama in a relationship they never should have been in? Well, this is the same. Learn from others and save the grief.

You've absorbed a lot of information in these pages, don't stop or skip pages now. This is important stuff. The final story demonstrates how pricing your house right the first time is crucial in a changing market.

UNDERPRICING, THE EASIEST WAY TO LOSE MONEY ON YOUR HOUSE SALE

The #1 reason people lose money on their house sale (as in, not getting all the money they could) is underpricing. They think their house is worth 'x' dollars without researching the value. They put their house on the market, sell it for less than it's worth, and never realize their mistake. That is why it's so critical you have a real understanding of the value of your house in today's market.

A perfect example is the sellers who sold three acres — worth about $500,000 — for only $280,000. They lived about 30 miles away and didn't realize the development potential the property had. They hired an agent who also didn't realize the development potential.

Their buyer was knowledgeable and experienced with developments. He researched the zoning and discovered the three acres were zoned for high-density condos. The sellers did not know about the zoning, nor did they know the county was planning to build a new road bordering their property.

You can see where this one went. In the end, the sellers were not aware they left $400,000 plus on the table until condo-building began.

BANK ERROR

Banks know that if a buyer makes an unsolicited offer, most of the time, the offer is below fair market value.
In one case, a bank lost more than $200,000 on a mis-
take based on that assumption. Two people were interested in buying a piece of property. It was in an excellent
location and unique among properties available in the
area. Both buyers were anxious to make an offer before
someone else could offer more. It was a so-called "pre-
forclosure."

Either one of them would have been willing to pay the
fair market value of $500,000 for the property. Money
was no problem; both buyers had the ability to pay in
cash. Unfortunately, the bank refused to take any offers
on the property. They would not budge until it was listed
on the open market. For some reason, possibly due to
an oversight, they put the property on the market for
$300,000.

First, the bank underpriced the property by
$200,000. Second, the hired agent didn't market it prop-
erly. Errors were made in the MLS listing. As a result, it
did not show up in search results for other agents who
had buyers looking for that type of property. The address was incorrect. As a result, the listing did not show
up on any of the real estate websites that use a map
display. Finally, the agent neglected to put a sign on

the property. (The person who eventually bought it lived down the road and drove past the property every day.)

After the bank refused to work with the buyers, each waited for the listing to appear. When it didn't show up in searches, they gave up. Ultimately, both buyers moved on to find other pieces of land. Meanwhile, the property sat on the market, unnoticed. Because of the agent's errors, no interest was generated, and the property went into default.

The man who lived nearby knew the bank had been trying to foreclose on the property. He did some research on the foreclosure at the courthouse. He found out the bank had successfully foreclosed on it. Knowing it had to be listed somewhere, he went online and searched through all of the properties for sale until he found the listing. To his surprise, it was priced well below the market.

Had the bank and agent not made mistakes, the two originally interested buyers would have made offers and likely started a bidding war. There is a good chance the two buyers would have driven the price up to the fair market value.

Most bank-owned properties are priced below market for a reason. Banks will discount houses they sell because they sit empty for months, and the banks typically have no knowledge of their condition.

The bank missed a full-price sale and lost $200,000. The property was acres of raw pasture. There were no unseen problems with it. The buyer had lived down the road from it for years and was very familiar with it. He submitted their asking price, and the bank accepted it. He saved $200,000 because the bank's agent didn't perform well and substantially underpriced the property. The bank suffered a significant loss.

ERRORS IN PRICE ADJUSTMENTS ARE COSTLY

There are times when pricing adjustments may need to be considered. For instance, let's look at Tim and Sue's situation.

Comparable House A: $768,000
Comparable House B: $749,000
Tim and Sue's House : $745,000
Comparable House C: $745,000
Comparable House D: $733,000
Comparable House E: $729,000

Tim and Sue appear to have priced their house competitively for the market. Over the next month, the market changes.

Comparable House A: Expired
Tim and Sue's House : $745,000

Comparable House B: $739,000 (Reduced Price)
Comparable House C: $735,000 (Reduced Price)
Comparable House D: Sold
Comparable House E: Pending
Comparable House F: $726,000 (New Listing)
Comparable House G: $725,000 (New Listing)
Comparable House H: $719,000 (New Listing)

Tim and Sue now have the highest priced house in the area in their price range. When a buyer looks at the comparable house prices, it is now the worst value proposition in the marketplace. Most sellers, like Tim and Sue, do not realize the market can shift so far so quickly. Examine the pricing trends and the direction. This can also happen in reverse. It cannot be stressed enough how important it is for you to price your house right the first time. House D sold, and House E had a pending sale from the start.

HOUSE SALE "HORROR STORIES"

Any real estate transaction can go awry. Out of ignorance, fraud, money laundering, mischief, fake money wiring requests, or larceny, issues can arise to complicate selling the house or cost the seller money. Having a real estate professional involved in the transaction will provide knowledge, somewhere to turn, and action.

Pre-closing Error: Buyers Moving in Too Soon

An agent-represented house owner was selling a house owned in a small town in Washington State. She accepted a buyer's offer, moved, and was awaiting transaction's closing.

The seller found out that the buyers were moving in before the date of closing. Seller called her agent, who contacted the buyers' agent and noted that the buyers should not have had the keys and definitely should not be moving into the house. (There are several legal, insurance-related, and ownership reasons for this). The buyers told their agent that they thought it was all right to move in before closing; it's not!

While the buyers did not get to move in early, they did transfer the utilities to their name well before closing. The agents worked together to explain that the buyers could not turn on the utilities in their name until escrow closed.

"I don't think they ever really understood why, but thankfully they did comply," the seller's agent said.

Fraudulent Buyers

A real estate agent was working for sellers whose house had sat unsold for several months. They were thrilled to get a cash offer for the $600,000 house from a couple. The buyers offered a proof-of-funds letter from a brokerage firm. The buyers' extended family turned out for the house inspection. It was like a holiday open house.

Later, the brokerage informed the agent that the proof-of-funds letter had a forged signature. The would-be buyers vanished, but the agent reported their extended family verbally abused her, the sellers, and the buyers' agent. Who knows why people do things. The agent now makes sure she verifies proof of funds and pre-qualification letters.

Houses Not Researched

In a transaction without the involvement of real estate agents, a woman purchased a rural house. She found out two years later, at the time she went to list the house, that it had once belonged to a person who was in jail for producing methamphetamine onsite! The revelation also obligated the house owner to take the necessary steps of decontaminating the house and ensuring it was fit for resale, costing her a whopping $16,000 in the process.

Pressure to Sell from Your Own Agent

House owners were selling a starter house in Washington D.C., circa late 1990s. They were asking $235,000. When they received a $226,000 offer with buyer demands that they cover $6,000 in closing costs, their agent prodded them into strongly considering the offer. Ultimately, they sold for $228,000 while honoring the closing cost request at the behest of their agent. Pre-housing crisis, houses in this neighborhood were selling for between $650,000 and $700,000. "In hindsight, I felt that I'd been negotiating against three people—the buyer, his agent, and his own agent," said the seller. This is no way for a seller to feel. As a seller, no matter what thoughtful advice you receive, don't forget, you make the final decision. Right or wrong, you are the one who has to live with it.

Preclosing Error: Large Bank Deposit Causing Delay

A couple buying a seller's house deposited $8,000 in cash into their checking account three days before closing. Their father had given them money to buy new furniture and appliances for the house. Their mortgage company checked balances the day before and it was "dinged," as it required a gift letter. The father had just gone to the UP of Michigan for a hunting/fishing trip and no one could reach him. This delayed the closing by two weeks. Large deposits is something to consider not doing, too near closing day.

WHY SHOULD THESE STORIES MATTER TO YOU?

Do you see how important it is to know the true value of your house? Moral of the story: Anyone can lose money in the real estate market. A seller unfamiliar with the ever changing market risks selling the house for less than it's worth or losing a sale because of incorrect pricing at listing. In most cases, sellers never even realize it. Pricing errors happen to private sellers all the time. Knowing the house's true value protects you from settling for less money.

9

Finding Precious Buyers

You now understand the importance of pricing and how real estate today is largely driven by technology. How do you find buyers? The two most valuable tools for finding ready buyers are the previously covered strategic pricing and an aggressive online marketing plan.

According to recent National Association of Realtors® surveys, 76% of house buyers first found the house they purchased on the Internet. Zero% found houses in the local newspaper; 9 of 10 house shoppers use the Internet to search for properties using syndicated realty websites.

Your house can be seen from anywhere; however, you shouldn't rely on exposure alone. Smart agents will feature your house on websites directed at buyers. Website search functions should filter results by using criteria such as schools, neighborhoods, and subdivisions. Buyers look for a house in a place that fits their lifestyle. The dedicated website should provide a wealth of information to buyers regarding proximity to schools, shopping centers, restaurants, and entertainment. This is an excellent way to find interested buyers. When a buyer is deciding where to live, you want your house included in the search results.

A neighborhood consisting of senior citizens and retired people, without a designated school bus stop close by, would not suit a family with school-aged children, even though the house might meet their other criteria. A bachelor may not be interested in living near children, even though a two-story house with a garage is what they're looking for. By design, websites should direct buyers to houses that meet their lifestyle, thus eliminating uninterested shoppers.

GIVE YOUR HOUSE A "YOUTUBE" TOUR

A YouTube tour shows the buyer your personal perspective of living in the house and can be linked to most major search engines. If you choose to do this, be proactive about getting the video out there. Send links of the video to any interested parties and make sure your real estate agent is doing the same. Insist that your agent get it on his or her company's website.

Further, make sure that, in this Information Age, you utilize marketing vehicles beyond traditional Realtor networks. Two out of three house buyers start their search online. The top highest-traffic websites are:

Realtor.com	LoopNet.com	RealtyTrac.com
Movoto.com	Redfin.com	HotPads.com
Zillow.com	Trulia.com	Homes.com

If you are unable to do proper marketing for your video, ask your real estate agent to do it for you, it is a partnership, and everyone should do the most they can to get the job done; both agent and seller.

Your best option is to discuss aggressive online marketing with a real estate agent who would like to list your house. You want to assure yourself that the agent has modern social media plans and outlets. You want to maximize your exposure as well as generate interest from your target market.

The CMA will help you price your house strategically, and your online presentation should bring you interested buyers.

10

Be A Power Negotiator

Negotiating your house sale does not have to be intimidating. By learning how real estate negotiations work and how to apply proven techniques, you can get the price you want from the buyers.

KNOW MORE THAN YOUR BUYERS

The two major elements of negotiation are motivation and skill.

- A motivated buyer wants the best deal, and you, the seller, want the best price.
- A skilled negotiator is an expert at working under the pressures of competition, time, information, and communication.

WHAT MOTIVATES A SELLER

- · Time on the market
- · Relocation
- · Pressures of maintenance and upkeep
- · Emotional and mental stress, especially during divorce or other trauma

Selling your house is a multifaceted process. To be a strong negotiator, you must avoid allowing emotions to overpower the situation to the point where you compromise and settle for a lower price.

Worrying about paying the mortgage while the house sits on the market for six months or having to move out of state are prime pressure points for sellers. Maintaining a house in showing condition for months on end can physically wear someone down. For some sellers, finding the right buyer can be mentally and emotionally straining. Knowledgeable buyers will push to the limit to get the price they want.

WHEN THE COMPETITIVE PRESSURE IS ON

When facing an informed buyer, remember that the party with the most options will win the negotiation. The buyer may have researched your house's history on the market. If you have relocated, he may assume that you're desperate to sell and will take his offer. On the flip side, if he thought you had three other buyers waving higher offers, he would have to raise his price or walk away. Sharpen your senses to know when a buyer does not have other property options.

Perceptions have a profound influence in negotiations. If an interested buyer believes you have rejected offers that were higher than his, you have the upper hand to pressure him to offer more. On that flip side, the buyer may inform you that he is interested in other houses, pressuring you to accept his price. The key to being a power negotiator is to stay calm and focused during the process to avoid costly mistakes. Knowing your buyer's motivation without exposing yours will give you an edge.

LET TIME BE ON YOUR SIDE

Time pressure is inescapable in the world of sales. It is evident during antique auctions, construction job bids, and car sales. Time is a powerful negotiation tool. Real estate agents advise buyers that a seller under pressure to sell will provide the best bargain. For this reason, smart house shoppers will obtain as much information about the seller as they can get, especially from a chatty Seller during a house showing.

For example, if a buyer knows a seller is in foreclosure and must sell before losing the property, the buyer has the upper hand. He knows the seller is under a time constraint and will use that, making low-ball offers or perhaps appearing indecisive or by not promptly returning calls and messages.

Buyers look for time-sensitive situations to push their price. Sellers who are behind on mortgage payments, recently retired, or are under contract for another house dependent on this house sale are candidates for high-pressure tactics from savvy buyers. Buyers may come to you and ask questions to find out if any of these situations apply to you. Eagerness to please them may be read as desperation.

Buyers also play the waiting game. In real estate, acceptance time can be a powerful tool in price negotiations. From their perspective, the longer the house has been on the market, the more flexible the seller will be. The same applies to negotiations. The more they stretch out the time spent in negotiating the sale, the more likely they will get the price they want.

Buyers will invest time with you to create relationships, trust, and willingness on your part to agree to their terms. The advantage that may arise for you is that they may not want to walk away empty-handed after gaining your trust. By exercising patience, you can maintain your position on terms and price.

** Tip **

Be a decent human & buyer/seller. Try to get what you need but remember, all business is not good business. You may win being an amoral negotiator, but you will lose in the long run. There is a situation where everyone is happy and everyone wins.

KNOWLEDGE IS POWER

Information is the key to real estate negotiations. The more information the buyer can glean from you, the more pressure you will face. Of course you can always say no, but the more knowledgeable side will overpower the less informed at the bargaining table. The more insight the buyer has into your motivation to sell, the more powerful he is at negotiating.

Don't avoid questions. Don't be unfriendly or uninterested. However, remember this is a professional transaction between strangers and don't be unnecessarily forthcoming, either.

When the buyer asks what appears to be a tough question that may relate to an offer, she is looking for direct answers and your *reactions*. Stay professionally reserved and avoid showing anxiousness to sell.

A simple but effective technique to handle a tough question without giving out information is to answer with another question. If you are asked if your house has been long on the market, simply answer imprecisely, e.g., "Not long." Then calmly ask the shoppers how long they have been looking. Their answers may empower you with information about their own stress points.

When asked why you are selling, answer with vague reasons, such as downsizing or eliminating stairs. Again, turn the tables by asking them the same question. To learn if you have any time constraints, a buyer might ask how soon you want to move. Tell them you're flexible, even if you would really like to move immediately. Next, it's your turn to ask them how soon *they* want to move. You never know what pressure one is under.

Directing the question back to the buyer maintains your control of information. What you paid for your house does not have a bearing on current market value, so if the question comes up, simply smile and say you won it in a bet (knowing the buyer has probably checked county records for the previous sale price).

Facing questions on the pricing of your house should not be difficult if you have put serious thought into your asking price. If you based it on professional market value estimates, tell them. Do not forget to point out recent sales of comparable houses and the improvements you've made. Competitive offers from other interested buyers are a concern for a house shopper. If they ask you about this, briefly state that there is interest but "nothing on paper." Don't be specific about where you are with other prospective buyers.

Buyers may be inquisitive as to why your house has not sold yet, and you can tell them you are waiting for the perfect buyer (like them!). Almost invariably they will ask for the lowest price you will take, or if the price is negotiable. Let them know you had not much time to think about it. In turn, ask what price they had in mind, adding "as long as the offer is negotiable."

Dealing with the buyers, keep this objective in mind. Answer questions thoughtfully but vaguely, without revealing much. Managing your responses by asking them questions in return works well in the situations discussed above. Always attempt to get the other party to reveal their thoughts.

On a side note, some real estate agents will want information from the listing agent. If a buyer agent contacts your agent, he may be looking to exchange sensitive information to get the sale. Have a discussion with your agent so you can be on the same page in all phases of the sale.

11

The Do's and Don'ts of Negotiating

Selling your house is a business transaction. Although it may be a many-layered process that appears more personal than business, at its heart, it's simply a buyer negotiating to purchase a seller's house for an agreed-upon price. You as a seller must keep this fact in mind. Opinions, emotions, and ego may attempt to derail your efforts; don't be the transgressor.

The more you know about negotiating, the less likely you are to create a needless detour during the sale process. Avoid offenses, biases, prejudices and all sorts of unnecessary wrongs. Be a decent human and get the deal done.

DO LET THE BUYER SPEAK FIRST

Let patience be your guide when dealing with an interested buyer. Don't be anxious to tell him or her what you're willing to accept; it may be lower than the buyer was willing to offer! Like any sale transaction, buyers have a price in mind, even if it is a lawn mower at a yard sale. They might be willing to pay $200 for the mower, but when they ask, you say $125. Do not lose the advantage of being able to counteroffer rather than offer first. Let the buyer speak first. That's why it's called an offer. It will either be an offer you can accept - or you will at least have more knowledge about what price the buyer has in mind.

DON'T "MEET IN THE MIDDLE"

Even in the simplest of sales transactions, agreeing on a price often includes "meeting in the middle." For instance, a buyer speaks first and offers to buy an item for $150, when the seller is expecting to sell for $200. Most will split the difference and counteroffer $175. By keeping the splitting point in the seller's favor by counteroffering $220, the mid-point is now $200. The buyer may take the offer or agree to $205, which is slightly more than what the seller planned to ask for. Maximize your negotiating by counteroffering in small increments. Avoid following human nature or the buyers choice of "meeting in the middle."

DON'T ACCEPT LOW-BALL OFFERS

House buyers look for deals. Think how quickly you would jump at a house selling below market value and in perfect condition that meets your every need. That situation rarely happens, but that doesn't mean buyers won't make low-ball offers. If they see your house as the perfect house, they may switch their priority to getting a lower-than-market-value price in negotiations. If buyers truly like your house better than any others, then why would they pay less for it? Keep focused and negotiate accordingly.

> *"talk less, smile more,*
> *don't let them know*
> *what you're against or*
> *what you're for"*

In this case, Aaron Burr is correct. Whether you are approached by the buyer or the buyer's agent, remaining quiet is one of the best ways to negotiate the sale. Developing a feel-good, overly friendly relationship with either can interfere with your focused efforts to sell your house quickly and for a fair price. Buyers uncomfortable with your quietness may want to break the silence by giving information that would be crucial to know. Again, the more knowledgeable you are about the buyer — rather than the other way around — the better poised you will be in negotiations.

DON'T BE MOVED BY AWKWARD SILENCE

When you are negotiating and the buyer makes an offer, don't feel compelled to respond immediately. Whether it be 10 seconds, 10 minutes or 10 hours, make the buyer or his agent speak first. They may see your silence as disappointment and choose to revise the offer or offer a concession just to break the silence. If you have to, hold your breath. Look at your phone and wait. Think of it as a silent contest; let them speak first. Do not let experienced negotiators use this tactic to get you to accept successively lower offers without a counteroffer from you and your agent.

DO LEARN WHAT MOTIVATES THE BUYER

Sometimes buying agents will work to learn why you want to sell your house. Agents know that sellers want to go to escrow only once. If the buyer is advised to demand a lower price because of minor defects discovered during a third-party house inspection, they will use this as a negotiating tool.

More importantly, an agent for the buyer may advise his client to offer the asking price, knowing that minor flaws exist, only to demand reductions bringing the offer down to what the buyer wanted to pay.

This is especially true when the house needs a lot of work and has been on the market long. If a buyer can get you in escrow, then when you are salivating from the completion of a long sale, the buyer hits you with the lower price that you are likely to take.

Knowing that situations like this happen, don't let the process of selling your house wear you out. Don't compromise your time and effort to keep things moving in escrow. Your listing agent should suggest a house inspection before you list to avoid trouble when negotiating the sale.

** Hot Tip **

Get a property inspection and a Termite report before listing. Get the important things fixed so there are no issues and you won't get suckered into negotiating down because of unknown issues with the house. It will take a little more time but save you money.

DON'T FREELY GIVE OUT YOUR INFORMATION

If you have multiple offers on your house, the price is not always the bottom line. Sometimes what you tell the buyer is advantageous to his/her offer, rather than your selling position.

For example, let's say you have two interested buyers. One buyer offers full asking price, thinking that you will readily accept, but tells you she needs a few months to close to get financing finalized or to get inspections. The other buyer casually asks why you are selling, and you offer crucial information about a coming transfer that leads the buyer to offer $10,000 less than your asking price but agrees to close quickly without any financial or inspection contingencies.

While the first buyer offered more money, the second buyer was more appealing time-wise. If you were under a time constraint, the second buyer solved your problem.

How did he know about the time constraint? You may have disclosed it without thinking when he asked why you were selling AND the buyer saved him or herself and extra $10,000! (and you lost yourself an extra $10,000).

DO GET THE LAST CONCESSION

Remaining calm and focused during counteroffers is the key to getting the last concession. By asking the buyer to give something in return every time he comes back with another request, you gain the upper hand, and he will start backing away from making nonessential demands. The less he thinks he can get away with, the less he will ask for beyond what he really needs. He may be afraid you will request a concession that is important to him and come to understand that letting you have the last concession will be his best deal.

DON'T BECOME FLOODED WITH CONCESSIONS

When a buyer submits an offer to you, unless it's a fantastic one, you should bring counteroffers to the table. Perhaps a different price and/or concessions — such as shorter closing dates, terms, modifications of contingencies, or incentives — will enter the negotiations.

When reviewing the offer, be sure to consider items that would be unacceptable to you. A counteroffer is used to, in effect, accept some (or most) of the terms of the buyer's latest offer, while modifying other items. Since there is no limit to the amount of times counteroffers can be made, make sure the buyer will have to wait for your response. Your eagerness to respond may be interpreted as desperation on your part, which, in turn, may give the buyer more leverage.

DO MAINTAIN A BUSINESS DEMEANOR

Remind yourself that you want to sell your house for the best price and in the shortest time. Seller/buyer relationships come in all shapes and sizes, but no matter what ensues, selling your house is a legal, documented, court-recorded, I's-dotted-and-T's-crossed business transaction. People do not get emotionally involved when buying a bag of oranges, but house selling does have a way of sneaking into one's emotions and triggering negative responses.

If the buyer has an inflated ego and acts like a know-it-all, you need to make sure it does not affect you. On the flip side, if the buyer comes off as the sweetest, kindest, but somewhat financially troubled person you've ever met, do not let that dissuade you from your goal of getting a fair deal.

Stay on your toes, even if the sale is going along quickly and painlessly. Sometimes it's an indication that the buyers might back out of the deal. There needs to be a certain amount of discussion by both parties to keep the buyer from jumping ship or, on your part, feeling seller's remorse. You may sense afterward that the buyer would have been willing to pay more for your house.

DON'T LET YOUR EGO GET THE BEST OF YOU

During negotiations, there may be a time when you think of all the labor and time you have invested in getting your house sold. Hours upon hours spent cleaning, staging, showing, and communicating may suddenly flood your mind. This is normal, you worked your butt off an it doesn't feel appreciated.

You may wonder if it was in vain when faced with buyers who are critical, demanding, or rude. Retaliation in like manner can break a deal, so learn to deal with potential house buyers objectively. Don't let your ego get in the way of a good deal.

12

Know Your Bargaining Chips

Selling is the name of the game. In the previous negotiation chapters, we learned that counteroffers by potential buyers sometimes include certain personal property, like appliances and window treatments, because these items are must-haves that are expensive to purchase new.

As a seller, you can use extras as bargaining chips as well. You may make counteroffers that include appliances and other contents as incentives for the bidder to agree to a higher price. This is a particularly useful strategy when the demand for houses in your neighborhood is weak and prices are low.

When you're selling your house, consider what you are willing to throw in to sweeten the deal, and what items are "off limits."

Here are some items you may want to consider using as leverage:

- Major appliances: washer, dryer, fridge, stove, dishwasher
- Draperies, curtains, blinds, and shutters
- Custom-built furniture: bookcases or shelves that fit a particular spot in the house
- Area rugs that fit a room
- Barbeque Grill or Garden shed
- Patio furniture: planters, garden benches, and ornaments
- Lawnmower, power washer, leaf vacuum, or other maintenance equipment
- Recreational equipment, such as ping-pong and pool tables, above-ground pools, trampolines, climbers, swing sets, and hot tubs
- Offer to prepay taxes or closing costs
- Offer a year of landscaping, pool cleaning, or maid service
- Offer that car you've been wanting to get rid of

The decision-making process is relatively simple if you consider what items you are willing to part with based on how easy or difficult it will be to move them. Also, consider how often you use movable items and the cost of replacement.

You can offer many kinds of incentives. A buyer may request an incentive in the transaction. It's all part of the negotiation. You can say yes, no or maybe.

Buyer requests or seller incentives may include:

- Reduction of the asking price
- Seller-paid points
- Help with the down payment
- Help with closing costs
- Let them stay in the house for 60 extra days
- Live in the house with you till they die
- Include that rusty classic car in the garage
- Offering to close in a short time
- Offering or transferring a house warranty
- Prepaid property taxes for one year
- Payment of HOA fees or landscaping and pool maintenance

The list is as long as your agent is creative, so discuss each of these with your listing agent before agreeing with a buyer.

NOTE: There may be restrictions placed on the real estate agent because of agency laws. There are also lender limits on buyer credits, and they MUST be properly disclosed, so be sure to stay within the limit of the laws.

KNOW WHY HOUSES DON'T SELL

Houses that do not sell for extended periods of time are usually priced too high or are too pricey for the neighborhood. Strategic pricing will always be the top reason houses sell successfully.

Here is a list of other common reasons that houses do not sell:

- The house is too cluttered. Piles and stacks of stuff discourage buyers.
- The house interior is dated. Old colors and old flooring deter sales, and so do any upgrades necessary to freshen up the decor.
- The house owner is not flexible with showings. Plan ahead to ensure kids, pets, and you are ready to show at any time and leave if you can.
- The market is not favorable at listing time. Deciding to list at another time may be the best option.
- The house is located in an abandoned development. The housing crash of 2008 left many houses empty in many neighborhoods.
- The real estate agent did not provide a sufficiently aggressive marketing plan.
- The real estate agent did not perform the Comparative Market Analysis correctly and failed to provide strategic pricing for the house.

13

Why Hire A Real Estate Pro?

This book is full of information on how to sell your house; it's almost everything you need. You have a basic knowledge of setting a listing price, online marketing, staging, and negotiation. Isn't this enough to do the job yourself? House owners wonder if they could buy or sell a house through online or traditional marketing and advertising channels without a real estate agent.

Try this analogy. You probably know I was a Series 7 Stock Broker with a major firm, back in the day. Imagine I gave you a book on investment strategy for your birthday and you read it. The stock market is at all-time highs, but there are political, business and do you remember Covid-19, factors that roil the markets. There are weeks of 900-point gains and of 1,500-point losses.

The question: Are you ready to handle your own Individual Retirement Account (IRA) or stock market investing? Do you have the expertise necessary, and can you handle the emotional roller-coaster of seeing thousands of dollars of your money come and go?

In today's realty market, the selling and purchasing of a residential property involves more than 100 people with different skills and expertise who participate in the transaction from start to finish. Whether it's for a house inspection or a title search, it takes more than 20 steps to finalize the sale of your house.

For sellers, it can seem overwhelming to know how to anticipate and coordinate every step necessary to prepare your house to show, list, market, and sell. An experienced real estate professional knowledgeable in all phases of real estate can make the process much easier. You do not need real estate expertise if you engage a professional who has it.

No matter how long you have lived in your house, a real estate professional in the local area will know considerably more about the sale price history and market trends than you do. Since real estate agents are paid a percentage of your selling price, it's in their best interest to price it perfectly. They want to earn the highest commission possible, but they also want to earn a commission within a reasonable amount of selling time. If it takes a year of time and expense, your agent might get tired and frustrated, just like you will.

Real estate agents' network with various contractors and professionals. They can advise on service providers' reputation and provide references who have previously worked with providers. Agents either possess intimate knowledge about your area or they have the contacts and resources to find the necessary information. They can identify comparable sales, in addition to pointing you in the direction where you can find more data on schools, crime, or demographics to provide potential buyers.

For example, you may know that a house down the street was on the market for $750,000, but a professional real estate agent will know the house had upgrades and sold at $685,000 after 65 days on the market.

A real estate agent will also have market conditions data, which will affect your selling process. Many factors determine how you will proceed. Data such as the average per-square-foot cost of similar houses, median and average sales prices, average number of days on market, and comparisons of list-to-sold prices will have a huge bearing on what you ultimately decide to do.

Attempting to sell your house without an agent requires a major effort, resources, and countless hours understanding and organizing all the work. Professional agents' careers depend on their ethics and ability to build relationships with clients and the community they serve. Agents looking to make easy money rarely go to the effort of establishing a solid marketing plan or work at strategic pricing and usually are discount brokers.

There are many ways to find a good broker. Personal recommendations from friends and colleagues are often helpful. If someone outside the real estate business recommends up a broker, you can be pretty sure you are on to a winner. You want someone with energy, experience, enthusiasm drive and not someone too busy or "big," to give you the adequate attention you need and guide you through the whole process with both courtesy and professionalism.

Take the time to interview real estate agents in your area. Here are some traits to look for when hiring an agent. Is he or she:

A Professional? Here is a sad story. I remember one of my first houses sold. It was a tough transaction but because I was inexperienced, I cost my buyer $2,300 extra because I didn't check a certain box! I know now but still; a new agent should work with an experienced one or it could cost you in the end.

Current? Is the agent up-to-date with the latest housing trends so he/she can serve you effectively?

Hard worker? Is the agent more show than sweat? Does he/she hit the pavement and do the work or are they more of the fancy car and glitter "ivory tower" agent? You must decide which you prefer to get the job done.

Connected? Does the agent have the necessary contacts who can assist in every phase of selling your house? A network of connections includes house inspectors, quality service people, other brokers, and possibly county officials.

Knowledgeable? Is the agent familiar with the current market and able to price your house strategically? Does he/she know what is unique about your neighborhood to distinguish your house from the competition? Does he/she know what to highlight in your area to attract buyers?

Every Realtor (or Realtist) has an 8 digit identification number from the Department of Real Estate. The number can tell you approximately how long they have been in business. If the first two numbers start with either 00 or 01, you should be in good shape as far as experience goes.

Organized? An agent must pay close attention to your specific needs, communicate well, and be quick to follow leads. Do they have marketing already established?

Personable? Agents who are sincerely interested in helping you will "go the extra mile with a smile." They must be able to sell themselves to you as well as sell your house to a buyer.

Passionate? Some agents treat their job like a hobby or just a way to earn extra income. Find an agent who is passionate about real estate and loves the job.

Tenacious? Successful agents possess a strong work ethic. They are efficient and take advantage of time-saving tools that help sell your house. Make sure they have energy to get out and get your house sold, no matter what it takes.

Honest? Professional real estate agents build their reputation on high standards of business practices. If they get a financial Felony or DUI for instance, they will lose their license.

Self-motivated? Real estate agents are commission-only business people. Successful agents work hard because if it benefits their clients and it benefits them.

Creative? Sometimes it takes creativity to properly showcase a house, develop engaging content, and negotiate a sale. An agent who can quickly address any marketing need is an asset to you.

Tech-savvy? Agents well versed in the latest technology for marketing houses should have a website, social media setup, user-friendly house search options, and quality presentations online with high-resolution images of houses, videos, and slideshows.

A professional real estate agent wears many hats. He or she must be proficient in marketing, negotiating, consultation, legalities, property taxes, and, most of all, gaining the trust of clients. An agent who will meet your specific needs is certainly worth the 6% commission he/she will earn, and you will benefit from the 94% you will earn.

Having an agent represent you in your house sale benefits you. Agents negotiate from a different vantage. Unlike most buyers and sellers, they can distance themselves from the emotional side of the transaction. Agents are more proficient in negotiating because conducting negotiations is a regular part of their professional work and because they are skilled by frequent practice. After all, it's part of the real estate agent's job description and training.

Good agents are not simply go-between messengers delivering buyers' offers to sellers and carrying counteroffers back and forth. They are professionals who are trained to advise their clients on options and consequences and then present their clients' case in the best light and agree to hold client information confidential from competing interests.

The real estate agent can be a buffer between seller and buyer, keeping the transaction professional and "at arm's length." This is important in the negotiations phase when emotions are liable to be at their highest. The real estate agent can further filter all those phone calls that lead to nowhere from bargain hunters and real estate shoppers.

Having a real estate agent available when the house is being shown is a distinct advantage for a few reasons. The agent will field the scheduling calls, arranging them for the seller's convenience. The agent may even show the house (but not be required to show it), saving that seller time investment. The agent fields the follow-up questions. In short, having an agent will lessen the seller's investment of time and bother, while encouraging serious buyers to immediately write an offer.

Handling real estate transaction paperwork is also a big boon to the seller. One-page deposit receipts were prevalent 40 years ago. Today's purchase agreements run 18 pages or more. That does not include the federal- and state-mandated disclosures nor disclosures dictated by local customs. Most real estate files average thicknesses from one to three inches of paper. A mistake or omission could land you in court or cost you down the road.

Speaking of down the road, even a smooth closing without complications can come back to haunt you. For example, taxing authorities that collect property tax assessments, document stamps, or transfer tax can fall months behind and mix up invoices, resulting in a snag. These may be hard to handle without knowledge of the systems.

A good real estate agent will deal with these issues. Questions often arise that were overlooked in the excitement of closing. A proficient agent will be there to assist.

Don't Sell Your House!

Don't sell your house until after you give all of the alternatives serious consideration. If you have outgrown your home, need to downsize or move out of the area, please consider first, not selling your house. I'm giving you advice I would give my mother and father; please take it.

If you have equity, you could borrow against it, buy somewhere else and rent out your house to cover the mortgage; and be in position for future appreciation because you still own. I know this is not always possible. You could let your adult children move in and help you out or rent it to a nice family until it's a better market and then sell if that's the issue. If you move out of state, you can have somewhere to come back to if snow, hurricanes, tornado's, fires or floods push you to change your mind. This is especially true if you are leaving California or New York. Because of the higher prices, it's not the easiest task to come back. That being said, do what is best for your situation.

The decision to sell your house requires seeing the total picture, from start to finish. You should now understand what is involved in selling your house quickly and profitably. However, let us summarize a bit about what you should consider to avoid trouble in the process. To eliminate any misunderstandings by you, your agent, or an interested buyer, discuss this list with your trusted agent.

- **Selling your house before you are qualified to buy another** — financial situations change along with loan requirements.
- **Guessing your mortgage payoff** — know if penalties exist.
- **Underestimation of closing costs** — calculate fees, taxes, and commissions that need to be paid.
- **Spending of earnest money** — if the sale falls through, what happens to the money?
- **Befriending potential buyers** — discretion is imperative when buyers want to be your friend.

- **Fear of low appraisals** — you have three options if this happens.
- **Stress of showings, remodels, cleaning, phone calls** — let your agent handle the bulk of the responsibilities of selling your house.
- **Facing inspection requirements** — know what is expected for your house to pass.
- **Being prepared for closing** — your agent and title company should let you know what to expect.
- **Flexibility and readiness to show your house** — make preparations so showings do not interfere with your family and your life.
- **Letting buyers see your house in your absence** — buyers prefer to view houses without the seller present to listen to their critiques. Any questions should be fielded by your agent.
- **Weeding out non-qualified buyers** — you can request that only qualified house buyers view your house. If they are not eligible, even for creative financing, it's a waste of everyone's time — especially yours.

Thank you for your time and attention. If you follow the suggestions offered in this book you will be on your way to a successful sales transaction. There is a lot going on in the country and world, the last thing you need is another something to worry about.

Stay safe, Stay healthy, Stay profitable.

Top Dollar For Your House?

Want Top Dollar For Your House?

There are many different things you can do to sell your house for top dollar. If you use these strategies, you get a higher sales price. But, miss any of these crucial components, and you risk settling for a lower price than you deserve. These are real dollars to you and each one counts.

Get a Free "Sell For Top Dollar" Consultation. Someone from my team will meet with you, take a look at your house, arrange an inspection for you and show you exactly what needs to be done to sell for top dollar.

You'll get advice on marketing, pictures, pricing strategy, staging and negotiations. Each of these items are crucial to your sale. Get them all right, and you'll sell for top dollar. Neglect one of them, and you risk settling for less than you deserve. Ask questions and move forward. Thanks for your time and good luck!

Sellers (and Buyers), you now know everything *you need to know* about selling a house; now stop making excuses, let go of your fears and go out there and make some money!

~ Donald Drake ~
The Art House Real Estate Group
DRE: 01256986 (since 1998)
Email:DDrakeRealEstate@gmail.com
Website:www.DDrakeRealEstate.com

Testimonials

Here's a couple of people whom I have helped buy or sell a house, and what they said about working with me:

"Donald had a tough job, but he did it!"

We were tough clients! We were moving to Nevada and didn't have a lot of time to look at houses, having to deal with our employer's relocation, and all of the other challenges that came along. But, Donald went above and beyond to help us. Even now, one year after the sale closed, I can still call him for business and service recommendations in the area — he knows just about everyone and is very happy to help.

"Donald Drake is the best agent in City!"

I've used Donald twice so far, and I was impressed both times. I bought my dream house with Donald 3 years ago. He worked long and hard to find me the perfect house. And he just recently sold another property of mine. Everything went quickly and smoothly. Both of my real estate deals were done very quickly and professionally. Donald is honestly the BEST in his business. I would highly recommend him.

"Donald's perseverance got me the house."

My experience with Donald during the entire house -buying process, from start to finish, has been nothing short of exceptional. I have a unique work structure, and because of this, it was very difficult to find mortgage lenders that would approve me for a house. I was very frustrated and on the verge of giving up, but Donald insisted that we continue searching.

Not only did we find a mortgage lender but also a mortgage that I felt great about. His perseverance is the reason I am now a house owner. He is professional, punctual, knowledgeable, and very easy to work with. With the highest regard, I will recommend Donald to all my friends and family.

"Donald kept us calm throughout the process!"

Donald always made himself available to answer questions. He worked hard to sell our house and find the best fit for our new house. He and his team worked with us through the entire process and kept us calm when we got anxious.

"I am 100 percent satisfied!!"

Donald Drake is professional and knowledgeable about everything. He is also always available. I would definitely recommend him to anyone. Very smooth transaction from start to finish. I felt confident with his experience.

"Donald found us our dream house."

Donald was very efficient and helped us find our dream house within a few short months. But when the Seller wouldn't move out, Donald told us to leave and he'd take care of it. I won't say what he did but I could not believe it and he got them out in one weekend! Incredible.

"Excellent experience topped with a personal touch."

Excellent experience all around, not only knowledgeable but Donald and team have a very personal touch. I felt like family throughout the entire process. He always took his time; we never felt rushed or like "just a number." I sold my house and bought with him. We had lots of questions, lots and lots of questions and he gladly answered them with no problem and guided us through the entire process, eliminating lots of stress. I truly appreciate that and would recommend him and his team to family and friends.

"Putting his clients (my family) above his own needs"

Donald found the perfect house as the sign was going up one morning. It was the lowest priced house with the best lot - in one of the best neighborhoods. He called me and offered the house to us first because it was everything we had also been looking for. He could have bought it for himself to live in but he called me!

He told me "if you don't buy this house, I will" and he meant it. That was a really BIG deal for him to pass up. What kind of a person does that? <>

www.ingramcontent.com/pod-product-compliance
Lightning Source LLC
Chambersburg PA
CBHW072137020426
42334CB00018B/1837